Ghillie Başan has written more than fifty books on different culinary cultures which, over the last forty years, have been shortlisted and have won a variety of awards. Her recent book, on Lebanese cooking, won Best in the World in the Gourmand International Cookbook Awards 2021 and *A Taste of the Highlands* was shortlisted for the Guild of Food Writers Award 2022. Her food and travel articles have appeared in a huge variety of newspapers, including the *Sunday Times* and the *Daily Telegraph*, and magazines such as *BBC Good Food* and *Delicious*. As a broadcaster she has presented and contributed to many BBC radio programmes and produces her own podcast, Spirit & Spice. Her book of the same name gives a unique insight into both whisky and food pairing, using wild and local produce combined with global spices, and Ghillie's extraordinary lifestyle in a remote part of the Scottish Highlands, where she runs cookery workshops and interactive whisky and food pairing experiences. Ghillie is also one of Scotland's Food Tourism Ambassadors and champions local produce.

SEAFOOD JOURNEY

Tastes and Tales from Scotland

GHILLIE BAŞAN

BIRLINN

First published in 2023 by
Birlinn Limited
West Newington House
10 Newington Road
Edinburgh
EH9 1QS

www.birlinn.co.uk

ISBN: 978 1 78027 832 2

British Library Cataloguing-in-Publication Data
A catalogue record for this book is available
from the British Library

Typeset by Mark Blackadder

Food and location photography © Lynne Kennedy

Additional photography credits:

p.i (author portrait) Christina Riley; 4: Euan Myles;
5: Samuel Hauenstein Swan; 23: Islay Sea Adventures;
43: Alistair Petrie/Alamy Stock Photo;
44: Alexander Mathieson; 53: India Hobson;
89: Laurence Winram; 90: Lewis Mackenzie;
112: Louis Neate; 120: Gordon Mackay;
126: Team Redshank; 152: Susan Malloy;
154: Charlene Storey; 192–3 & 227: Mike Guest;
224: Paul Watt.

Printed and bound by Bell & Bain, Glasgow

CONTENTS

ACKNOWLEDGEMENTS

The journey in this book follows the stories of people associated with the sea and our wonderful fish and shellfish around Scotland's coastline. It doesn't venture inland. Yet I live in the Cairngorms National Park and rely hugely on my fishmonger, Pro Fish Scotland, in the inland mountain-resort town of Aviemore. Born out of a random discussion at the dinner table one evening in 2017, Pro Fish Scotland has Lionel Raguenet at the helm. A former fisherman and, when he was 15 years old, the youngest recruit in the French navy, Lionel has 35 years of fish-filleting experience and has managed to pass on both his love of the sea and knowledge of the fishing industry to his wife, two sons, daughter and son-in-law – all of whom work in the business. Only the highest MSC-graded (Marine Stewardship Council) seafood is selected daily from the Peterhead and Shetland markets, then it is processed by Lionel's sons, Steven and Jimmy, in Dingwall and transported in mobile fish vans by Lionel and his son-in-law, James MacQueen, to remote areas of the Highlands and Moray, and sold in the shop in Aviemore. Along with several other fish vans from places like Buckie and Portsoy, Pro Fish provides rural, inland communities like ours with top-quality fresh fish on a daily basis. Most of the seafood for this book was sourced and supplied by Lionel's daughter, Stephanie, and his wife, Sylvie – two of the loveliest and most accommodating people you will ever meet. Nothing is too much trouble – the beautiful fish is always sold with a smile, and even a wee cooking tip if you need one. For the different events that we run, my daughter and I, along with many regional restaurants and cafes, rely on Stephanie and Sylvie, so my first big 'thank you' goes to the Pro Fish Scotland family. We are lucky to have you!

I would also like to thank all the characters in this book – from salt producers to fishermen, chefs and boat builders – who have shared their stories with me so generously. Their collaborative goodwill and passion for the fishing industry and our amazing seafood is a joy to share. I have learnt a lot on my journey and I have gained a profound respect for everyone involved, so my thanks come sincerely from the bottom of my heart. Amongst these characters is food writer Liz Ashworth, who introduced me to Orkney fishermen and fish merchants, and helped with the chapter on the Moray coast, and Gary Maclean, who agreed to write the Foreword, somewhat in the dark, but who is a passionate national ambassador of Scotland's seafood.

My thanks also go to the ever-patient managing editor of Birlinn, Andrew Simmons; the editor, Debs Warner, who expertly steered the final stages of the book's photography and design; the designer, Mark Blackadder, who had to chop and change at my whim but has come up trumps; Anita Joseph, the most helpful and skilled copy editor I have ever worked with; and to my literary agent, the one and only Jenny Brown, the best agent and friend an author can wish for.

I reserve my final thanks for Lynne Kennedy, who took the majority of the photographs for this book. She is a skilled wedding and documentary photographer but this was her first food project. I wouldn't have asked her to come on board if I didn't believe in her and she proved to be a dream to work with. I hope that this book gives her a platform to shine in the way that she deserves. I would happily work with her again in a heartbeat!

FOREWORD

Gary Maclean
SCOTLAND'S NATIONAL CHEF

As a chef, educator and food ambassador, I have been promoting Scottish food at home and abroad for over 30 years, serving the great and the good in the most wonderful locations all over the world and showcasing our produce and food traditions from Singapore to Los Angeles and everywhere in between. The more I travel, the prouder I become of my homeland.

I am particularly fascinated with Scottish fish and shellfish. So much so, I was inspired to open my own seafood restaurant, Creel Caught, after watching the trucks queuing up at Dover as we tried to export our catch into Europe at the beginning of Brexit. I felt that I must do as much as I could to support the industry.

Being a Scottish chef who has worked predominantly in Scotland, it wasn't until I started to travel and cook in other countries having to use non-Scottish produce that I realised how good our fish and shellfish was. I remember doing a Scottish showcase in a very high-end restaurant in Los Angeles. The delivery of seafood had just arrived and the executive chef started to unpack it. His reaction to the quality and standard was amazing, the best he had ever seen. The fish was so good, he actually started carrying samples of it around the kitchen to show it off to the other chefs. It was an incredible experience for me to see food from my country being revered by others and, in a way, seeing our food through their eyes.

Much of my career has been in further education working at the City of Glasgow College teaching the next generation of chefs. I have always felt that it is important as an educator to give as full a picture of the industry as possible. Helping learners understand the food chain and the importance of careful procurement is vital. What I have also seen in the last few years is that new students are asking a lot of questions on provenance and welfare and how their future buying affects the planet. It shows how far we have come in a short space of time.

I have been very lucky in my career to have been able to promote our incredible food in every corner of the world. It's an easy sell if I

Josh Talbot (p.101) loading boxes of langoustines into the Keltic Seafare van (p.121) in Ullapool.

am honest. A chef working in a quality establishment anywhere in the world knows that to have the word 'Scottish' on his menu shows that they are the best. As I write this, I am waiting to board a plane to Delhi, to attend yet another showcase of our incredible food and culture. I realise that, in Scotland, we are doing something different. We don't stack it high and sell it cheap, we purely focus on quality. Every plane- and truck-load of Scottish fish and shellfish that leaves our country is telling the story of who we are, one box at a time.

INTRODUCTION

The last holiday my children and I had with my parents was on Tanera Mor, the largest of the Summer Isles off the north-west coast of Scotland. My father, who was in his late eighties at the time, had seen an article in the newspaper about the new island owner who had renovated some of the cottages to rent.

My father had fond memories of his honeymoon there; my mother didn't. In fact, I'm surprised they remained married. The boat had dropped them off at the old, disused herring station with a Border terrier pup that had been given to them as a wedding present and the skipper said he would pick them up the next day. My father had brought my mother to the island to camp and pitched the tent on the only bit of flat grassy ground near the harbour. He was in his element. He had always camped as a boy and, ever since travelling the world as the doctor on a Blue Funnel Line merchant ship, he had developed a love for the sea, boats and fishing. A wild storm began to brew, but he was in the water looking for crabs to cook for his new wife. My mother had never camped and the heavens opened with such torrential rain that their tent was flooded and hundreds of earwigs took refuge on the inside which kept Tinker, the pup, busy as she tried to eat them. Adding to my mother's misery, the boat couldn't return to pick them up for four days.

My children and I helped my elderly father walk along the path from the cottage to the old herring station so he could show us where they had camped. They laughed at my mother's dramatic account of her miserable honeymoon – one could laugh because my father did redeem himself the following year by taking her to Venice and they remained happily married for 56 years – and were keen to see where he had pitched the tent and to look for crabs. Arriving at the roofless herring station which dates back to 1784 and the little harbour created for the boats to land the fish, my father told my children about the glorious days of the herring boom that began in the late 1800s and lasted until the early nineteenth century.

It was an extraordinary moment in Scotland's fishing history, heralding the construction of harbours, herring stations and saltpans. Salt was needed in vast quantities to preserve the herring in barrels that were transported to places like Germany, Eastern Europe and Russia. The fishermen would follow the shoals through summer months when they were at their fattest, around the Hebrides and the west coast, around Orkney and Shetland, and the whole length of the east coast. Young girls from the fishing villages, the 'herring lassies', would follow the boats to gut and pack the 'silver darlings' in the salt. It was hard, physical work and the girls had to make cloth bandages to try to prevent the salt from getting into the cuts and scratches on their hands. They were earning a wage, which was unusual at that time, and there was fun to be had with dancing and music and, in some cases, the meeting of future husbands. According to SCOSHH (scottishherring.org), by the 1900s, the Scottish herring industry had become the largest in Europe, producing over 2 million barrels and employing over 35,000 people.

Ten years after that holiday in the Summer Isles, I was hosting a group from Sweden on a Whisky Food Safari, a whisky and food pairing experience that I host at my home in the Cairngorms, and one of the tasters was a big, juicy, fresh scallop from the west coast. The leader of the group was delighted. He and several of his friends travel the world as shellfish enthusiasts and will go as far as Spain, California and Indonesia to get 'the best'. But the best is here, I enthused, and pointed out that the shellfish he had in Spain probably came from Scotland anyway. Regrettably, the Swede's past experience of Scotland's shellfish had been disappointing. He had visited the Isle of Skye and couldn't find any fresh shellfish, herring or cod. Admittedly it was a time when Scottish pubs and restaurants were all too comfortable with the deep-fat fryer and lumps of frozen prawn in breadcrumbs – scampi and chips, scampi and peas, and a sachet of ketchup or tartare sauce on the side. I don't know how we managed to sink from the glory of the herring days to deep-fried prawns but, I assured my Swedish guest, he would be blown away by the quality and freshness of our seafood now and we have some of the best chefs to prepare it.

During the pandemic years of 2020 and 2021, I was struck by a recurring conversation I had in several coastal communities. I was travelling up and down the west coast between the lockdowns,

writing my book, *A Taste of the Highlands*, and kept meeting locals who were enjoying shellfish for the first time. Some felt they were living like kings with lobster on the table several times a week; others were unsure what to do with it. All of them had been used to the landed catch from the waters around Mull, Skye and Ullapool being loaded straight onto lorries heading to London, France and Spain while they bought haddock, prawns and dressed crab from the fish vans that came all the way from the east coast. It is a dynamic that is difficult to comprehend, with laws and quotas regarding what a boat can and cannot land.

So, when I started writing this book, I had these locals in mind.

At the end of filming *Appetite for Adventure* (p.96), we enjoyed Cape Wrath Oysters (p.117) on the beach in Durness.

Bally Philp (p.84) on his boat, *Nemesis* BRD 115, Skye.

In Scotland, we have more coastline than any other part of the UK. Seafood is one of our biggest exports, and while it is important to showcase Scotland as a global seafood destination it is also important for those of us who live in Scotland to enjoy eating more fish and shellfish and to be inventive with it. Since the pandemic and Brexit, there have been positive changes for the home market as some fishermen and fish farmers have switched to selling solely to the local communities and restaurants whilst others are holding back enough for locals before the rest goes to export. The raft of guidelines and quotas often don't make sense to the fishermen, especially when they see premium fish ending up as bait. The recurring conversation I was having while writing this book, two years later, switched to boats going out of business and the industry dying due to unrealistic regulations. Most fishermen go to sea because they love it and see it as a way of life, they said, but the fun was being sucked out of it.

On my journey around the coast I gained such respect for our fishermen and cemented my appreciation of the quality of our seafood. In my imagination, I followed in the wake of the herring boats and herring lassies, starting in Ayr in the south where the wind is being harnessed to produce salt from the seawater, to the Western Isles, up the coast to Orkney and Shetland, and down the east coast to Fife and East Lothian to meet people whose lives are associated with the sea. I met not just fishermen, but salt producers, shellfish farmers, seaweed harvesters and foragers, creel makers, boat makers, fish merchants and several seafood chefs. The resulting stories provide a potted picture of our coastal communities today, the challenges they face and the lives they lead in order to provide us with the wonderful products of the sea.

There are some traditional recipes amongst the modern and multi-cultural ones. They reflect the society we live in and the way we often draw inspiration from different culinary cultures and our own travels. All the recipes in the book are easy to prepare and have been written with the intention of inspiring you to have a bit of fun with our glorious fish and shellfish. Whether seared in a little butter with salt and pepper and a squeeze of lemon, or cooked in a spicy broth or a soulful curry, you simply can't go wrong when the quality of the seafood is so fresh and so good!

Ancestral Coastal Survival

Before heading off on our seafood journey, I thought it would be interesting to hear how our ancestors would have survived by the sea. They would have been skilled foragers and fishermen; they would have understood the seasons and the tides; they would have produced salt and preserved fish in it; and they would have cooked fish over fires and tanned the skins to make leather for shoes and pouches. Many of these ancient skills are being practised again today, so I have asked Patrick McGlinchey, the founder and director of Backwoods Survival School, and the ancestral skills consultant and practitioner for a number of BBC programmes to paint a picture of our ancestors' lives for us.

The remains of shell middens scattered throughout Scotland give us an insight into some of what they consumed in ancient times, by hugging the shoreline and utilising the resources of the woodland environment in which they thrived. It was a smart strategy, the best of both environments. A day actively hunting in the forest could yield nothing and use up valuable calories whereas a walk on the shoreline would offer them abundant protein without much effort. They were literally standing on their next meal. Working with the ebb and flow of the tide they would gather their daily needs from this living larder and also forage for the seasonal edible and medicinal plants that grow on the shoreline above the high-tide mark.

You'll find many different habitats on the coastline but it's the estuaries and rocky shore that yield the rich pickings as far as foraging is concerned. Looking out onto an empty beach at low tide would give you the impression that there was nothing to gather but you'd be wrong, the tell-tale signs of food are everywhere. Empty shells, small holes and strange mounds of coiled sand will indicate what you may find when you dig below the surface: a delicious array of bivalves await the persistent forager – cockles, razor clams, oysters, sand gapers and other tasty clams can be gathered.

The rugged and rocky shoreline offers so much more diversity and goes beyond what would be called survival food. It's buzzing with an incredible array of life. Most of the brown carpet will be made up of the wrack family, such as bladder, serrated and spiral, which occupies the rocks on the upper and middle zone to the water's edge. Everything that exists on this exposed shore has a survival strategy, called 'hold on'. The violence of winter storms would deposit everything onto the land, but the wracks and other seaweeds have evolved to cope with this and anchor themselves to rocks with a strong holdfast. Other delights you may find in this zone are the red and green seaweeds like carrageen, dulse, laver, gut weed and one of my favourites, sea lettuce. Amongst the rocks and wracks you'll also find limpets, top shells, whelks, mussels, periwinkles, dog whelks and other tasty goodies. Foraging after a storm or spring tide you may find some confused scallops pushed and thrown higher up the shore – a real treat with freshly gathered

sorrel. Shellfish, conveniently, come in their own pot and contain enough water to cook them when placed on the hot coals of a fire.

Early people had an intimacy with nature and their surroundings. As well as foraging, they crafted different styles of funnel traps made from flexible saplings like willow for catching shore crab in great numbers, and creels could be dropped into deeper water for larger crustaceans like lobster, brown crab, velvet crab, prawns and squats.

They manufactured harpoons, nets, hooks and lines that would allow them to spear and catch fish. The communal effort of creating and using nets, which could be made from many different kinds of natural fibre, could feed the whole tribe and allow for the excess to be preserved by smoking or salting for the leaner times. And early watercraft allowed the people access to the open sea and deep water, enabling them to hunt sea mammals and birds. These early boats could have been made from flexible saplings, which were bound and woven like a stretched-out basket and then covered with mammal skins sewn together with sinew and sealed with fat. A few years ago I made a skin boat similar to this description and it successfully crossed from mainland Scotland to Orkney carrying nine people.

Above left. Patrick McGlinchey in his element with freshly caught mackerel.

Above right. Traditional harpoons made by Patrick McGlinchey.

I
West Coast

The championing of local seafood begins right at the south-west foot of Scotland, with the annual Oyster Festival in Stranraer celebrating the fishing heritage of the region. This heritage includes the winter spawning of herring off the Ayrshire coast and the skirmishes amongst fishermen in the mid 1800s over the ring netting of the abundant herring in Loch Fyne, an area now known for its seafood fine dining. Off the coast of Ayr and Argyll, there are seafood shacks on the Isles of Bute and Arran, hand-dived scallops, farmed oysters, whirlpool sea salt on Islay and an award-winning smokehouse on Mull. The coastal road winds past trout and salmon farms through Oban, around Ardnamurchan to Arisaig, and on to the busy harbour of Mallaig, once an important herring port but later Europe's largest prawn port.

Blackthorn Sea Salt (Ayr)

Until around the sixteenth century, Ayr was the biggest producer of salt in Scotland. With the demand for large quantities to cure and brine the herring in the seventeenth century, the salt producers of the east coast became more organised and slowly the Ayrshire pans became redundant, the last closing in 1874. Now, Gregorie and Whirly Marshall have brought salt back to Ayr by trickling seawater down through a tower of blackthorn branches.

Saltpans Road leads to the harbour and will take you to the Blackthorn Tower with Goatfell and the jagged summits of the Isle of Arran in the distance. It is a structure of great beauty, standing tall, bold and formidable, as if bracing itself to withstand the wild, west-coast gales whipping off the sea at its feet. Up close, it is an architectural wonder, 8 metres high, 25 metres in length, and fashioned out of thousands of intricately woven blackthorn branches stacked at a slight slant. Inside, the wonder continues, with a staircase leading up through the larch and Douglas fir skeleton to a bolted trap door through which you can access a rooftop platform. Outside, it can appear dark and brooding in the mist and rain; inside, the shafts of light can lend a sacred atmosphere enhanced by the tuneful sound of trickling seawater and whistling wind.

As I stand and admire the structure, my mind fills with questions. I ask the fundamental ones first. How did they come up with this idea? And how does it work?

Gregorie, the Master Salter, tells me that in the 1800s his great-great-grandfather founded the family importing business, Peacock Salt, so he has salt ancestry in his blood and has been involved in it all his life. But Gregorie himself trained as an architect. Aha! That accounts for the high tower and attention to detail, but it took him 12 years of research, trials and errors to create this natural structure, which mirrors in miniature the medieval rock salt graduation towers of Germany and Poland. In the early years, those structures were built stacked with straw, but they rotted and fouled the brine. Eventually blackthorn bushels were selected for their hardiness and longevity, lasting seven to ten years before needing to be replaced. Those towers are no longer used to produce salt and have mostly been converted into spas, but their construction gave Gregorie food

Above. The impressive Blackthorn Tower, with Arran in the distance.

Opposite. The Blackthorn Sea Salt producers, Gregorie and Whirly Marshall.

for thought when he visited them in 2007. The first batch of Blackthorn Sea Salt Flakes was harvested in 2019.

The process is so well thought out, it appears both simple and magical as 26,000 litres of pristine seawater is pumped through a filter into a holding tank and then dribbled into the tower through 54 wooden taps. This is the 'mother liquor' and it is often Whirly's job to monitor the flow. The blackthorn branches are thorny, which stretches out the surface area for the seawater to seep along and trickle down, exposing it to the coastal wind which accelerates the evaporation of the droplets, concentrating the brine. The aim is to evaporate the seawater down to 2,000 litres of concentrated brine with 22 per cent salinity, which Gregorie proudly monitors with his refractometer. This concentrated brine is filtered into two pans, which are like big baths. Where the liquid touches the air, small cube-shaped sodium chloride crystals begin to float on the surface. As they get

4

heavier gravity pulls them down under the liquid and the cubes stretch down into inverted pyramids, which slowly become heavier and sink to the bottom of the pan. These crystals are gathered into a large colander to drain for three days and any leftover brine, which is full of magnesium, goes back into the tower. To finish off the crystals and prevent clumping, they are warmed in an oven for around 90 minutes. The resulting product is a fine fleur de sel – delicate flakes rather than chunky crystals, slightly off-white in colour due to the tannins in the blackthorn branches. On the palate, the mineral-rich flakes echo soft notes of the sea with a slight umami hit from the blackthorn. For those lucky enough to visit the tower, Gregorie and Whirly have refurbished an old train carriage for tastings and events – a nod to the history of the area and the port's original bustle and industry, with wagons carrying coal and salt to and from the pans along the Ayrshire coastline.

Fire-cooked Mackerel with
Blackthorn Sea Salt and Chimichurri

Serves 4

———

For the chimichurri

a small bunch of flat-leaf parsley, finely chopped

a small bunch of fresh oregano, finely chopped

a small bunch of fresh coriander, finely chopped

1 fresh red chilli, deseeded and finely chopped

2 garlic cloves, crushed

2 tbsp red wine, or sherry, vinegar

125ml olive oil

1 tsp Blackthorn Sea Salt

freshly ground black pepper

———

2 medium-sized, or 4 small, freshly caught mackerel, gutted and cleaned

a handful of Blackthorn Sea Salt

———

For serving

mini tortilla wraps

4 tbsp homemade, or shop bought, mayonnaise, mixed with the zest of 1 lime or 1 tsp chipotle paste

Somewhere in the region of Loch Fyne, Patrick McGlinchey (p.xv) runs his Beachcomber and Coracle Building courses and, as he has told me that a magical meal for him is mackerel straight out of the sea, cleaned and cooked over a fire, or hot-smoked over coals, I have prepared this recipe with him in mind and added a bowl of herby, garlicky Argentinian chimichurri to dip them into. Set up your fire in a sensible location on the beach and prepare sticks by removing some of the bark and sharpening one end to a point.

———

To make the chimichurri, tip the chopped herbs, chilli and crushed garlic into a bowl. Stir in the vinegar, then pour in the oil gradually, stirring all the time so that it becomes thick. Season well with the salt and pepper and put aside to let the flavours mingle. Just before serving, give it a stir and adjust the flavour to taste with vinegar, olive oil or seasoning.

When your fire is ready, rub some salt over the mackerel and inside the cavity. Push the points of the sharpened sticks down through the mouth and into the body and stab the other end into the ground beside the fire at a distance that enables the fish to cook but avoids the skin charring too quickly. The cooking time will vary from 20 to 40 minutes, depending on the size of your mackerel and the heat of your fire in the outdoor elements.

Once cooked, you can enjoy the mackerel with your fingers by pulling back the skin and dipping the flesh into the chimichurri and mayonnaise, or slit them open, remove the fillets and serve with the sauces in the wraps.

Salt Cod with Aioli

Serves 6–8

1.5kg fresh cod fillet, or other fish, with skin on

Blackthorn Sea Salt

For the aioli

4 plump garlic cloves

Blackthorn Sea Salt

3 large egg yolks

3 tbsp olive oil

juice of ½–1 lemon, to taste

freshly ground black pepper

Salting cod was once a tradition, along with drying it, to preserve it for use in the winter months. Herring got a similar treatment. But it doesn't have to just be cod – you can, in fact, salt and dry most white fish and use it in similar ways. Many cultures around the world do this and the intensified flavour of the fish is integral to the dish. So here is a way to salt your own cod, or other fish, at home. I'm using Blackthorn Sea Salt but you can use any of the other wonderful sea salts produced around the coast. The whole preparation of this dish takes two days.

Run your fingers along the fish to check for bones – if there are any, pull them out with tweezers. Find a dish or container to fit your fish and pour in a layer of salt to cover the base. Place the fish, skin-side down, on this bed of salt and then completely cover with another layer of salt. Cover with cling film or foil and pop in the fridge for 24 hours.

Take the fish out of the fridge and lift it out of the brine that has formed from the salt. Rinse the fish in cold water then place it back into the cleaned dish or container and cover completely with cold water for 24 hours, changing the water three or four times.

After the salted fish has soaked in the water, drain and pat dry. It is now ready to poach, steam, roast, fry or add to a stew. If poaching, add white wine to the stock, and serve the cooked fish with home-made aioli.

To make the aioli, crush the garlic with a little salt and stir in the egg yolks. You can do this using a mortar and pestle, or a small bowl with a wooden spoon. Gradually add the olive oil in a thin stream, beating all the time, until your mayonnaise is nice and thick. Add the lemon juice gradually, adjusting to your taste, and season with the black pepper.

Otter Ferry Seafish (Loch Fyne)

When you have spent over three decades creating a premium product that is sustainable, traceable and delicious, but, for a number of reasons including cost and climate change, you have to let it go, the blow must be hard to bear.

Back in 1991, Alastair Barge, the owner and managing director of Otter Ferry Seafish, began a halibut hatchery on Loch Fyne as a way to reduce the pressure on the endangered wild stocks. He and his team took on the task of catching the broodstock in the North Atlantic waters around Iceland, the Faroes and northern Scotland and transporting them back to Loch Fyne where the cold temperature and algae of their natural habitat had to be simulated in the land-based tanks pumped with seawater. It was by no means an easy task but it was successful and the juveniles were transported to more land-based tanks on the Isle of Gigha where they continued to grow under the care of the local island team. From the annual harvest of 100 tons of fresh, healthy halibut, some were smoked over whisky barrel chips to produce the award-winning Gigha Smoked Halibut. But, recently, one of the problems that Otter Ferry Seafish has had to face is the rising temperature of the sea around the island affecting the viability of the farm and so the production of halibut on Gigha will have to end. This is the blow that is hard to bear.

With the blow comes resourcefulness, however. Alastair will look at alternative species that may be more suited to the changing conditions around Gigha, and the halibut marine hatchery on Loch Fyne will continue to produce juvenile halibut to be transported to colder waters. Meanwhile, the ongoing production of wrasse to deploy to the salmon farms as cleaner fish keeps the team at Otter Ferry Seafish very busy. Once hatched, the wrasse are no bigger than an eyelash and require a complex diet to develop. They take 18 months to grow big enough to be deployed and, during this time, they have to acclimatise to the conditions of the salmon pens in order to reduce the stress of the transfer and maximise their performance as cleaner fish. By farming wrasse, Otter Ferry Seafish will hopefully release the pressure on the wild wrasse being caught as cleaner fish for the salmon tanks.

Halibut Kebabs with Orange Zest Chermoula

Fiery and zesty, chermoula is a classic Moroccan marinade for flavouring fish and chicken cooked in tagines and over the charcoal grill. The sweet, juicy flesh of fresh halibut is delicious marinated in this zingy, orange zest version and cooked over a fire bowl or charcoal grill. You can, of course, use any firm and chunky-fleshed fish of your choice, such as monkfish, ling, coley or salmon but, with great faith in Otter Ferry Seafish (p.9) finding a new home for the rearing of their juvenile halibut, I am thinking ahead.

———

Using a mortar and pestle, pound the garlic and cumin seeds with the salt to a smooth paste. Pound in the orange zest to work the natural oil, then stir in the orange and lemon juice. Add the olive oil, chopped chillies and herbs, and mix well.

Place the halibut chunks into a shallow bowl and spoon the chermoula over them. Gently toss the chunks in the chermoula, making sure they are coated. Cover and chill for roughly 6 hours so that the flavours penetrate the fish.

Prepare your outdoor grill, or fire bowl. Gently toss the halibut chunks one more time to make sure they are coated in the chermoula and thread them onto the skewers, alternating with a piece of pepper in between every two or three chunks of halibut.

Place the skewers over the grill, or fire bowl, and cook for 2–3 minutes each side, until firm and just cooked.

Enjoy with lemon or orange wedges to squeeze over them.

Serves 6–8

———

For the chermoula

4 plump garlic cloves

1–2 tsp cumin seeds

1 tsp Blackthorn Sea Salt

grated zest of 2 oranges

juice of 1 orange

juice of 2 lemons

1 tbsp olive oil

2 fresh red chillies, deseeded and finely chopped

a small bunch of fresh coriander, finely chopped

a small bunch of flat-leaf parsley, finely chopped

———

1 whole side of halibut, roughly 900g, trimmed and cut into bite-sized chunks

2 bell peppers, perhaps 1 red, 1 yellow for colour, deseeded and cut into modest bite-sized pieces

metal skewers

lemon or orange wedges, for serving

Halibut Fillets with
Jura Journey Beurre Blanc (Jura)

Serves 2

---

1 shallot, finely chopped

170g butter

60ml whisky

50ml double cream

a squeeze of lemon juice

a glug of olive oil

2 thick halibut or hake fillets with skin on and patted dry with kitchen paper

sea salt and freshly ground black pepper

Jura Journey, to accompany

The ferry ride from the mainland over to Islay and Jura only takes a couple of hours but it feels like a world away from the mainland. If you arrive in Port Askaig on Islay, a tiny car ferry takes you the short distance across the Sound of Islay to the Isle of Jura. Here, the single road snakes along the shoreline and through open moorland, passing wild deer and glimpses of the stunning Paps, to the island's pub, whisky distillery, gin distillery and the new distillery for Deer Island Rum. 'Deer Island' is understood to be the meaning of the Norse word jura which is apt as there are estimated to be 5,000 red deer and only 250 inhabitants on the island. With its unspoilt feel, Jura is one of my favourite west coast islands, and home to one of my preferred whiskies, drawing its pure water from the tops of the Paps. You could use any of the Jura single malts for this recipe but the Jura Journey, matured in bourbon casks, with its creamy, nutty, soft spice and pear notes, is a good place to start.

Melt roughly 20g of the butter in a small saucepan. Stir in the chopped shallot to soften. Tip in the whisky to deglaze the pan and burn off the alcohol. Add the cream and simmer to scalding point, but don't boil.

Keep the saucepan over a low flame and gradually add bits of the butter, making sure each bit melts into the cream before you add more. Be careful to keep the pan moving and at an even temperature – if the cream gets too hot the butter will separate.

When all the butter has been added, stir gently while you add in a squeeze of lemon juice. Season to taste and splash in an extra spoonful of whisky.

Keep the beurre blanc warm while you quickly pan-fry the halibut fillets. Heat your pan over a medium heat, add a glug of oil and, when it gets hot, place the fillets, skin-side down, in the pan. Sear the fillets for 3–4 minutes, then flip them over and sear for another 2 minutes. Flip them back again so that the skin is underneath and season with salt and pepper. Slip the fillets onto plates, serve with the Jura Journey Beurre Blanc and pour yourself a dram to go with it!

Lussa Gin Scallop Ceviche with Pickled Sea Lettuce (Jura)

Lussa Gin Distillery is located about 25 miles from the ferry at the north end of the island on Ardlussa Estate, where three women produce a deliciously fresh and zesty spirit with a hint of rose. Georgina is the distiller, Alicia is the business head and Claire, who is married to the estate owner, is in charge of sales and marketing. The crystal-clear spring water comes from the estate and almost all of the gin's 15 botanicals, such as lemon thyme, honeysuckle, scented roses, bog myrtle and sea lettuce, are foraged or grown locally. Lizzie Massie, who grew up on Ardlussa Estate and lives nearby, cooks for guests at the estate lodge and uses the gin in her recipes. She usually serves this scallop ceviche on blinis as a starter.

Place the sea lettuce in a bowl. Stir the sugar into the vinegar and pour it over the sea lettuce. Leave to marinate for about 20 minutes then drain and cut into thin strips.

Just before serving, use a very sharp knife to finely slice the scallops. Lay the slices in a shallow dish and pour over the gin and lemon juice. Leave them to soak for 1 minute.

Lift the slices out of the gin and arrange them on blinis or oatcakes. Sprinkle each one with a little sea salt, chopped chilli and chives, and garnish with the strips of pickled sea lettuce. Serve immediately.

Makes roughly 20 canapés

For the pickled sea lettuce

a handful of sea lettuce, patted dry with kitchen paper

2 tsp caster sugar

100ml wine vinegar or rice vinegar

4 large scallops

50ml Lussa Gin

½ lemon

Orsay Sea Salt (p.16)

½ fresh green chilli, deseeded and very finely chopped

2–3 chives, finely snipped

blinis or oatcakes, for serving

15

Orsay Sea Salt (Islay)

The Isle of Islay feels less rugged and less wild than Jura but it is a very bonnie island with its coastal villages built around whisky distilleries, most of them whitewashed and quaint with vast stretches of peaty moorland in between. Currently, there are nine working distilleries on Islay, drawing in visitors from all over the world, particularly during the Fèis Ìle, a week-long festival of whisky, music, culture and seafood. At one time whisky and fishing would have been the main forms of employment and the houses built around the distilleries would have been lived in by the workers and their families, but when I drove out to Port Wemyss and Portnahaven, two neighbouring, whitewashed villages separated by a burn on the southern tip of Rhinns of Islay, I was struck by their emptiness. It was October and it was dusk, so the night was drawing in, but there were only a few lights on here and there. The majority of the houses in these two villages are holiday homes; the locals simply can't afford them. Anna Hock, the founder of Orsay Sea Salt, is one of them. Without the generosity of a local crofter, also a fisherman, who has gifted the use of his land for the salt tunnels, Anna wouldn't be able to run her business and plan for the future. She and her husband would like to stay on the island and build a house for their family one day.

Anna would be great at running Sea Salt Tours, one of her future plans, as she loves taking people around the rocky shoreline of Port Wemyss to tell you about her small organic business, Orsay Sea Salt. She began experimenting with the evaporation of seawater in her kitchen when her children were babies and the more she experimented, the more she became intrigued by the difference in mineral content and taste depending on where the seawater was collected from. The best results came from the most dangerous spot – a whirlpool called 'the kettle' where four strong tides converge on the far side of the lighthouse island. This interesting discovery means that her courageous husband, Ashley, a local crab and lobster fisherman who grew up by these waters, has to go and collect it. He knows how to time the tides for his trip into 'the kettle' with two 1,000-litre containers on his boat. Once he has filled them, he returns to the slipway at Port Wemyss and transfers the containers to his

truck so that he can drive them up the hill on to the croft land where Anna has two polytunnels erected for the salt production.

In order to tick all the food-safety boxes, Anna has the clean seawater filtered twice manually – first from the sea into the containers and then when it is pumped from the containers onto the floor of the main polytunnel. The water is then left to evaporate under the natural heat created by the sun and once crystals form they are transferred to the second polytunnel to dry on shelves. Two tons of seawater produces 100 kilos of sea salt which perfectly captures the taste of the pristine sea – a purity that has led to two exciting partnerships: one with Ardnahoe Distillery producing a 'malted salt' and the other with Beinn an Tuirc Distillers in Kintyre to make a 'salt vodka' called Earra Gael. Anna's labour of love is the first of its kind on Islay and, although Orsay Sea Salt is still in its infancy, it is exciting to see that distilleries and locals are supporting her.

Orsay Salt-roasted Langoustines

Roasting or baking fish and shellfish in salt is an age-old tradition and enhances the sweetness of the flesh. When a whole fish is encased in salt and baked in the oven, the salt bleaches the flesh as well as enhancing the sweetness and when you remove the hardened baked salt casing it takes the skin with it. With langoustines I prefer to roast them in the salt over a fire, or a gas flame, so that you can see them change colour and gauge when they are ready. You need enough sea salt to cover the base of the pan you are using and you need to get it hot before placing the langoustines on top. The chunky Orsay Sea Salt crystals are described as 'a pinch of island life' on the jar but you will need much more than a pinch! Both the natural and malted salt will work well.

Serves 2

———

roughly 350g natural or malted Orsay Sea Salt

12 langoustines kept at –1°C to stun them into hibernation before cooking

aioli, for serving (see p.8 for recipe)

Place a heavy-based pan over the fire, or a gas flame, with a thick layer of salt covering the base. Once the salt gets hot, place the langoustines on top and cook for 5–6 minutes, then flip them over and cook the other side.

The langoustines will be ready when they turn opaque but you can check by lifting one out with tongs and snapping the tail away from the head to see if the flesh is cooked.

Use your fingers to shell them and dip into aioli or a flavoured mayonnaise of your choice. Enjoy the sweet juiciness of the flesh.

Islay Oysters in Crispy Oatmeal
with Garlicky Oyster Mayonnaise

Serves 4–6

For the mayonnaise

2 large Islay oysters, shucked and drained but keep the liquid

juice of 1 lemon

2 garlic cloves, crushed

2 egg yolks

300ml olive oil

Orsay Sea Salt

6 tbsp medium oatmeal

2 tbsp dry, day-old breadcrumbs

2 tsp ground pepper dulse

1 tsp Orsay Sea Salt

4 egg whites

roughly 12–16 Islay oysters, shucked and drained on kitchen paper

sunflower or rapeseed oil, for frying

finely chopped parsley, for garnishing

Shucking oysters comes easily to Craig Archibald who farms oysters in Loch Gruinart, a tidal estuary on the north coast of Islay. He supplies thousands of Islay Oysters a year to Loch Fyne Oysters and to David Lowrie Fish Merchants (p.203) in Fife. During the Islay Whisky Festival he sells approximately 6,000 oysters over five days. He and his wife, Petra, have taken over the family farm, which originally began as a cattle and sheep farm when Craig's parents moved to Islay from Yorkshire in 1971. His parents began Islay Oysters in 1989 as a farm diversification and discovered that the oysters grew well in the mild climate. The tide races into the loch twice a day and brings in fresh feed from the open sea, keeping the oysters fat and sweet and in tip-top condition. With so many deliciously meaty oysters to harvest all year round, the next step for Craig and Petra was to open a place for locals and visitors to enjoy them, along with their own lamb and beef. Housed in a converted stable, cart shed and byre, with a big window looking out over the loch, and Petra at the helm, the Oyster Shed has been an instant success. One of the most popular dishes is the crispy fried oysters in oatmeal with oyster mayonnaise. Delicious with an Islay dram!

To make the mayonnaise, blitz the oysters, lemon juice and garlic in a food processor. Add the yolks and blitz again, then add the olive oil in a slow, steady stream – as you would for ordinary mayonnaise – until thick and creamy. Beat in some of the reserved liquid from the oyster to achieve a consistency you are happy with and season to taste with salt. Tip the mayonnaise into a bowl and keep aside.

In a shallow dish, mix together the oatmeal, breadcrumbs and pepper dulse. Season with a little sea salt.

In another shallow bowl, whisk the egg whites until light and fluffy.

Gently pass each oyster through the egg white and roll in the oatmeal and breadcrumbs until coated.

Heat enough oil in a wok or deep frying pan to deep or shallow fry. When the oil is hot, fry the oysters until crispy and golden. Drain on kitchen paper and serve in the oyster shells, with a sprinkling of parsley and the oyster mayonnaise.

Opposite. Craig Archibald shucking his fresh oysters at Loch Gruinart, Islay.

Islay Sea Adventures' Hand-dived Scallops

I have such happy memories of my time with Islay Sea Adventures. I think if I lived on Islay I would want to work with this team as it exudes the hospitality of the Western Isles with warm banter and generous servings of whisky – it is a whisky island after all! I was with my daughter and, once we climbed on board, we were greeted with a fresh raw scallop each, bathed in Laphroig – a little peaty 'spirit' aid to help the scallop slide silkily down our throats as we tipped it from its shell. It could be said that, once on board the boat, the adventure begins with the business and boat owner, Gus Newman, and the skipper, Harold Hastie – a comedy duo who have years of experience as fishermen and members of the coastguard between them. Gus also dives for scallops and Harold cooks them.

Gus established Islay Sea Adventures in 2014 but has been in the charter boat business since 1999. He is a commercial fisherman, trained as a commercial diver in Fort William, and has been a member of the coastguard for 25 years. Harold is also a commercial fisherman and has been a member of the coastguard for 46 years. Also in the incredibly friendly team are Lori, who takes the bookings and organises the trips, and Hannah, who is the wildlife specialist and is learning to skipper the boat. There are wildlife trips designed specifically to spot harbour seals, sea eagles and pods of dolphins; there is the Corryvreckan trip which takes you to the famous whirlpool; and there is the seafood trip which takes you past Lagavulin, Laphroig and Ardbeg distilleries and on to Islay's Special Area of Conservation which is only viewable from the sea and where the waters are calm, so you can enjoy some of the freshest seafood imaginable in comfort.

With the boat rocking gently and the banter flowing, my daughter and I were presented with a platter of lobster and crab with chunks of fresh bread, salad and a bowl of homemade garlic sauce while the scallops went onto the boat's grill. Gus had dived for them that morning. His wetsuit was still dripping at the side of the boat. And Harold cooked them to perfection in just a little garlic and chilli butter. They were simply the plumpest, sweetest, juiciest scallops I have ever tasted, served with an Ardbeg dram. It doesn't get much better than that!

Opposite. Gus Newman and fresh, hand-dived scallops being cooked on board the Islay Sea Adventures boat.

Saigon Seafood Curry

Southern India and South-east Asia have many delicious coconut-milk-based seafood curries, but this Vietnamese version is one of my favourites because of the use of peanuts and basil leaves. You can use any combination of seafood you like and serve the curry with rice, noodles or chunks of crusty baguette – as they do in Saigon – to mop up the coconut curry sauce.

Using a mortar and pestle, pound the garlic, ginger and chillies together with the salt to form a coarse paste. Add half the peanuts, the coriander and lime zest, and pound to an almost smooth paste.

Heat the oil in a heavy-based pot and stir in the onion, until it begins to colour. Stir in the ginger, chilli and peanut paste for 2 minutes, then add the lemongrass, jaggery, shrimp paste, fish sauce and reserved lime juice. Once the aromas begin to tickle your nose, stir in the curry powder and coconut milk. Bring the mixture to the boil, then reduce the heat and simmer for 10 minutes. Season well to taste.

Bring the liquid to the boil once more and gently toss in the seafood, starting with the squid, then the scallops and prawns, and adding the white fish at the last minute when the prawns turn opaque. Gently toss most of the basil leaves through the curry, sprinkle the rest over the top with the reserved ground peanuts and serve immediately.

Serves 4

For the base paste

4 garlic cloves, roughly chopped

a large thumb-sized knob of ginger, roughly chopped

2 fresh red chillies, deseeded and roughly chopped

1 tsp Orsay Sea Salt

150g peanuts, roasted and coarsely ground

a handful of coriander leaves

grated zest of 2 limes (reserve the juice)

2–3 tbsp peanut, light sesame or vegetable oil

2 onions, roughly chopped

2 lemongrass stalks, trimmed and finely sliced

1 tbsp jaggery or light muscovado sugar

2 tsp shrimp paste

1 tbsp fish sauce

1 tbsp curry powder or garam masala

2 × 400ml tins coconut milk

sea salt and freshly ground black pepper

2 medium-sized squid sacs and tentacles, cut diagonally into 4–6 pieces.

roughly 8 shelled scallops

roughly 8 shelled prawns

2 fillets fresh haddock, cod, ling or coley, cut into chunks

a bunch of fresh basil leaves

Craig's Langoustine and Bruichladdich Bere Barley Brose with Sea Urchin Butter

Serves 4, or 8 as a starter

For the butter

8–10 very fresh sea urchins, to extract 40 roes

250g unsalted butter, at room temperature

150g white miso (or homemade miso)

10g sweet cicely, finely chopped

For the brose

100g unsalted butter

langoustine heads and shells (these will be left over from another dish so you may have 12, you may have 20)

240g onions, finely sliced

20g tomato paste

20ml Bruichladdich Bere Barley Whisky, plus extra to finish

30ml gooseberry or dry white wine

1 litre chicken stock

1 litre water

Blackthorn Sea Salt for seasoning, if needed

Bruichladdich Bere Barley Whisky, for accompanying

Glasgow-based Craig Grozier is no stranger to Islay. He has been collaborating with Bruichladdich Distillery and, in particular, The Botanist Gin for some time, sharing his knowledge of local and wild food with a variety of audiences and bartenders. I was staying at one of Bruichladdich's Academy Houses at the same time as Craig who had taken over the kitchen to prepare for a group of French clients. Lucky clients, I should add, as Craig, who is from the Highlands but has travelled to immerse himself in other culinary cultures and trained in top restaurants to refine techniques, is an extraordinarily inventive chef. He is also the founder of Fallachan Dining, which has a tasting menu to die for. So, it took a lot of restraint on my part to not dip a spoon into every sauce and preserve in the fridge and sneak off with one of his sea urchin and scallop roe combinations flavoured with wild horseradish and Bruichladdich malts. This was a showcase example of Craig's skill and ongoing relationship with Bruichladdich as he doesn't just cook with whisky, he incorporates every step of the whisky-making process – the malts, the wash, the draff – into his recipes and menus. For this recipe, he would normally make his own bere barley miso, which he prepares on Islay with barley malts, but he has suggested using a shop-bought alternative.

First make the butter. Cut each sea urchin from the mouth outwards into a circle to expose the roes. Pour out the liquid inside and carefully scoop out the roes. Rest them on a clean J-Cloth and remove any urchin spines. Blend the roes with the butter, miso and sweet cicely, then chill it. Once firm, dice the butter and keep chilled until ready to use.

To make the brose, melt the butter on a medium heat in a 5-litre heavy-based pot, until it starts to bubble. Toss in the langoustine heads and shells, until they smell aromatic and are caramelised, but not bitter.

Remove the shells from the pot and toss in the onions. Add more butter, if needed, as you want to lightly caramelise the onions. Stir in the tomato paste and lightly caramelise again. Deglaze with the

Craig Grozier on Islay.

whisky and wine, add the heads and shells back to the pot, and cover with the stock and water. Simmer gently for 1½ hours.

Strain the liquid through a sieve, then strain again through a piece of muslin and tip it back into the pot. Simmer the strained liquid until it reduces by half. (At this point you can leave it to cool and store in the fridge if you are not using it right away.)

Keep on a low simmer and, using an electric stick blender, add the sea urchin butter until it is light, frothy and creamy. Season with salt, if you think it needs it. Add the extra whisky you've reserved for the finish and blend and taste again.

Divide the brose amongst four bowls, or serve in espresso-sized vessels if serving eight as a starter.

Caledonian Oysters Rockefeller
with Aromatic Wild Herbs (Loch Creran)

Serves 4

4 spring onions, trimmed and roughly chopped

2 garlic cloves, roughly chopped

a handful of young rosebay willow herb leaves

a handful of sweet cicely leaves

a handful of scurvy grass

a handful of day-old white breadcrumbs

roughly 40g butter, at room temperature

a few drops Tabasco

sea salt and freshly ground black pepper

12 fresh Caledonian oysters

1 lemon, cut into 4 segments, for squeezing

The original recipe for the famous Oyster Rockefeller, which dates back to 1889 in New Orleans, is thought to have included spinach and parsley, possibly capers, in its green sauce, but there are now many variations on the theme. So, here's one of them, using oysters farmed by Judith Vajk at Caledonian Oysters in Loch Creran near Oban. She is a real champion of oysters and oyster farming and known throughout Scotland for her delicious Pacific and Native varieties, as well as her new venture in smoking oysters. Some of her Natives are huge but this recipe works best with her moderate-sized Pacific Oysters, which she now leaves in bags at her road end, like an oyster honesty box! In this recipe, I've placed the original spinach with young, wild rosebay willow herb leaves and added scurvy grass for its strong mustardy notes and sweet cicely for its aniseed flavour.

Shuck the oysters, place them in the deeper half of the shells and arrange them on a baking tray that will fit under your grill.

Blitz the spring onions, garlic, rosebay willow herb, sweet cicely and scurvy grass in a food processor. Add the breadcrumbs, butter and Tabasco to form a thick paste (add more breadcrumbs if necessary) and season to taste.

Spoon the paste on top of each oyster and place them under a hot grill for about 10 minutes, until crisp and golden brown. Enjoy hot, or at room temperature, with a squeeze of lemon or more Tabasco.

Smoked Oyster Omelette with Spring Onions and Stem Ginger

This is a great way to enjoy Judith Vajk's smoked oysters, a new addition to Caledonian Oysters. It is a popular dish in the food stalls of Singapore and Malaysia and you could easily substitute with smoked mussels from Andy Race (p.42) who smokes the plump ones from Arisaig Mussels (p.39). I would suggest enjoying the flavours with a peaty dram.

Heat the oil in a heavy-based frying pan. Stir in the garlic and chillies until they become fragrant. Toss in the spring onions to soften a little, then add the smoked oysters, preserved ginger and bean sprouts.

Stir in the soy sauce and mirin, bubble it up around the mussels, then pour in the beaten egg. Using a wooden spatula, pull the egg back from the edge of the pan, until it begins to set. Reduce the heat and cover the pan with a lid, or a sheet of aluminium foil, and cook gently until firm.

Drizzle a little chilli oil over the top and garnish with the coriander. Cut into wedges and serve immediately with a salad.

Serves 2–4

2 tbsp sesame or peanut oil

2 garlic cloves, finely chopped

1–2 fresh red chillies, deseeded and finely chopped

4 spring onions, trimmed and cut into 3 pieces

8 smoked oysters

1 preserved stem ginger, finely sliced

a handful of bean sprouts

2 tbsp soy sauce

1 tbsp mirin

8 eggs, lightly beaten with 2 tbsp milk

chilli oil or Tabasco

a small bunch of fresh coriander leaves, finely chopped

Tobermory Fish Company (Mull)

The Isle of Mull is known for its stunning landscape and wildlife, its historic sites and Tobermory's charming pastel-coloured houses, but it also has an outstanding food attraction. For generations, the award-winning, family-run Tobermory Fish Company has produced the most succulent and tasty products using traditional family recipes for cold smoking, or 'kippering' as it is also called (herring kippers have just adopted the name), and hot smoking, also known as 'smoke cooking'. Only Sally MacColl and her mum, Rosie Swinbanks, third and second generation, know the secrets of these traditional processes – the amount of salt and sugar and the aromatic herbs used – you can't even bribe the husbands or Sally's brother, as they remain in the dark!

The business began with Sally's grandparents in 1971, Hugh and Marjorie Goldie, and Sally is now at the helm. The refurbished premises has a delightful rustic vibe and is packed with seafood products – their own and others, prepared from products fished or gathered around the Hebridean islands, such as the seaweed chutney made by Tara Dixon McPhail who owns the local company, Isle of Mull Seaweed Chutney. You can also pick up all the sauces, dressings and vegetables you might need to go with your seafood, and you can buy Sally's pâtés and ready-to-pop-in-the-oven seafood dishes. She and Rosie are accomplished cooks and some of their favourite recipes are published in Sally's little slip-into-your-pocket book, *The Tobermory Seafood Bible*.

The journey over from the mainland – two ferries with long delays in my case – was well worth it as I stocked up on hot-smoked mussels, deliciously moist cold- and hot-smoked salmon and trout, smoked haddock and several tubs of homemade smoked salmon and smoked trout pâtés. Sally and Rosie love working together and their 'love' comes through in their products, which have reached the attention of many award-giving bodies and some of Scotland's biggest food ambassadors. Both Lady Claire Macdonald (p.70) and Gary Maclean (p.ix) praise the Tobermory Fish Company products very highly.

Tobermory Smoked
Trout and Horseradish

Serves 4

_____

2 spring onions, finely
chopped

½ cucumber, diced

25g fresh coriander, finely
chopped

200g cold-smoked trout slices

250g natural yoghurt

1 tbsp creamed horseradish

lime wedges, for squeezing

This simple dish is from Sally MacColl's book, The Tobermory Seafood
Bible, *and allows the Tobermory Fish Company's smoked trout to
sing. Simple and fresh, you can serve the smoked trout with brown
bread, as Sally suggests, or on oatcakes, blinis or Scots pancakes.*

_____

In a bowl, mix together the spring onions, cucumber and coriander.
Divide the smoked trout slices between four plates and heap the
spring onion and cucumber mix over them. Combine the yoghurt
with the creamed horseradish and pour it over the trout and salad.

Serve with the lime wedges to squeeze over it and chunks of crusty
brown bread and butter.

My Granny's Baked Smoked
Haddock and Cheddar Go-to

Serves 4

_____

4 smoked haddock fillets

300ml double cream

freshly ground black pepper

200g Isle of Mull cheddar,
coarsely grated

*This was my granny's fish supper 'go-to'. Simple and satisfying, all you
need is several fillets of smoked haddock, cream and a good cheddar.
It couldn't be easier but it is important that the smoked haddock has a
robust and sweet, smoky flavour. Here, I am using the Tobermory
smoked haddock with the lovely, tangy Isle of Mull cheddar. My granny
would serve this dish with steamed spinach or mashed potato but we
often have it for supper at home with a green salad.*

_____

Preheat the oven to 180°C (fan 160°C), 350°F, gas mark 4.

Lay the smoked haddock fillets flat in the base of an ovenproof
dish. Pour the cream over them and grind the black pepper over the
top. Scatter the cheese over the top and pop the dish in the oven for
about 20–25 minutes, until the cheese has melted and the fish has
cooked.

Serve the fillets immediately, spooning the flavoured cream over
the top and enjoy with a salad and chunks of bread, or with boiled
or mashed potatoes and steamed spinach.

Rosie Curtis (Ardnamurchan)

When Rosie Curtis gets up in the morning, she has hogs and tups to feed, along with 40 Blackface ewes, 4 Highland cattle and her son's hens to sort out while he's away at school. A scrub in the bath and breakfast sees her ready for a team talk at the office a short distance away and then she either goes out on site with the team, or she stays in the office to sort orders and records, and to watch the monitors. And while doing all of these things, she carries an emergency pager, which could go off at any time. She lives in a remote part of Ardnamurchan on the western tip of Scotland, where she is a mother of three, a crofter, chairperson of the community council, watch commander for the local fire service, deputy officer of the coastguard, *and* she has a day job as manager of the Mowi Salmon Farm at Maclean's Nose.

Working in the salmon industry had not been in Rosie's plans. She grew up on a croft in the small village of Kilchoan, went to Inverness to study and ended up doing a cooking course. This landed her a chef's job at the Nevis Range, the ski centre outside Fort William, where she worked for seven years. In 1997 her father was diagnosed with terminal cancer and she returned to Kilchoan to help her mother and look after the family croft. Her father died within the term diagnosed and, just as tragically, her mother died ten years later, so Rosie took over the croft, which had been left to her and her brother. As it is impossible to make a living from crofting alone, Rosie's husband worked at a local salmon farm with her brother and she took on the role of fish-farm technician at the Glenmore Fish Farm. They had three children and high childcare costs, so she and her husband agreed that he would stay at home with the children and run the croft while she climbed the ladder in the salmon-farm industry.

Twenty-five years on, and the only woman in her team, Rosie is one tough cookie. As manager, she is in charge of two teams of four on a two-weeks-on, two-weeks-off cycle and, along with her assistant manager, John, who is also part of the fire service and the coastguard, she keeps a watchful eye on the fish counts and health checks of over 1 million salmon in 16 pens. There are approximately 70,000 salmon in a pen alongside lumpfish and wrasse, the cleaner fish.

While it sounds like a lot of fish, the pens are very wide and deep,

so at maximum the pens contain 98 per cent water and just 2 per cent fish. Cleaner fish make up 10 per cent of the numbers in the pens and work in unison, picking skin parasites off the salmon; the lumpfish perform well in winter and the wrasse in summer. To reduce wild capture of wrasse and lumpfish, Mowi raises both species in specially designed aquaculture systems.

There are no hormones or dyes in the salmon feed, which is produced in Kyleakin on the Isle of Skye and is made up primarily of wheat, vegetables and fishmeal products with added vitamins and minerals. Every day one ton of feed is blown through pipes from a barge, up through a mushroom-shaped feeder and into the middle of each pen. While the salmon leap and eat their pellets dispersed by this sprinkler device, the cleaner fish hide in their artificial kelp forests, until the salmon are full and a different feed consisting of much smaller pellets is dispersed for them. If the weather is dangerously wild, this feeding process can be operated from the land-based office station that houses a display of high-definition monitors that are each linked to underwater and surface cameras.

I have to say I was impressed when I saw the set-up with my own eyes. Rosie took me out on her boat to see the fish in their 120-metre circular pens with 17-metre-deep nets and a bird net covering the top. The sea eagles overhead and regular appearances of curious seals and pods of dolphins don't give the farm team any cause for concern but the natural plankton and jellyfish blooms do. The plankton blooms form an oxygen-depriving wall around the pens and the rare jellyfish blooms also block the oxygen but, as they attach themselves to the nets, their tentacles split off and float into the pens and get into the gills of the fish. Another challenge for the fish is a gill infection, which occurs in the wild and presents itself as white spots. Rosie explained that wild salmon can only get rid of this infection by swimming from the sea into fresh water but, if the farm-raised salmon test positive for this infection, they undergo a harmless peroxide treatment or freshwater bath to get rid of it. She added that all health treatments are approved by the vets who visit regularly and by the various accrediting bodies and the RSPCA.

Out on the boat with Rosie in the open sea, watching her hop on to the swaying platforms surrounding the pens, it was clear that she was proud to be managing her thriving salmon farm reliant on cleaner fish in the tidal waters at the foot of Maclean's Nose. She is at her happiest when she is out with 'her' fish and she cares for them in the same way she cares for the animals on her croft.

If one of them is sick, she will immediately attend to it. And when it comes to the harvest, the process is humane – more humane than the slaughter of many pigs and cows. When the salmon reach approximately 5.5 kilos they are gathered in nets to be transferred to well boats in which they travel in seawater to Mallaig. There, they are pumped into the harvest station, still in seawater, and dispersed down individual pipes to be instantly stunned, bled and immediately chilled.

From there they are transported to Fort William to be gutted and packaged for their onward journey.

From the salmon farm at Maclean's Nose, 79 per cent of the fish remain in the UK, and are sold in leading retailers and online stores. Rosie makes sure that the traceability, sustainability, health and feed are transparent on the live documents she has to submit to Marine Scotland, SEPA and the RSPCA, and she is happy to handle the unannounced inspection visits and requests by interested parties to see what she does. One day, she would like to see the whole fish farming industry become accredited like Maclean's Nose and, with an ageing population of only 247 inhabitants in Kilchoan, Rosie hopes that the salmon farm will bring young people back to the community.

Ember-baked Salmon with Whisky, Juniper and Bog Myrtle

Serves 6

———

1 whole side of salmon (sustainably farmed and RSPCA Assured), roughly 1.5–1.8kg with skin on and pin-boned (you can ask your fishmonger to do this for you)

roughly 50g butter, cut into thin pieces

a handful of fresh or dried bog myrtle leaves

a handful of ripe juniper berries

a dram of whisky (choose one to suit your location)

sea salt

foil for wrapping

If I could, I would cook and eat outdoors all the time. Our Scottish weather means that isn't always possible so it becomes a real treat when I can. And once you have a fire on the go, there are ways to cook over it and in the embers. By wrapping a whole fish, or a whole filleted side, in foil with herbs and butter, and placing it on top of the embers to cook gently, you end up with beautifully moist and delicately cooked flesh – the most delicious way to enjoy a whole side of salmon.

———

Place the side of salmon skin-side down in a piece of aluminium foil large enough to form a parcel. Place the pieces of butter along the length of the side, scatter with the bog myrtle leaves and juniper berries, drizzle the whisky over the top and finish with a sprinkling of salt.

Pull up the sides of the foil to form a sealed parcel and place it flat on top of the embers. Depending on the size of your salmon side and the heat from your embers, the side of salmon will take 15–20 minutes to cook perfectly.

Gently pull the flesh away from the skin and enjoy with wedges of lemon, mayonnaise and a dram.

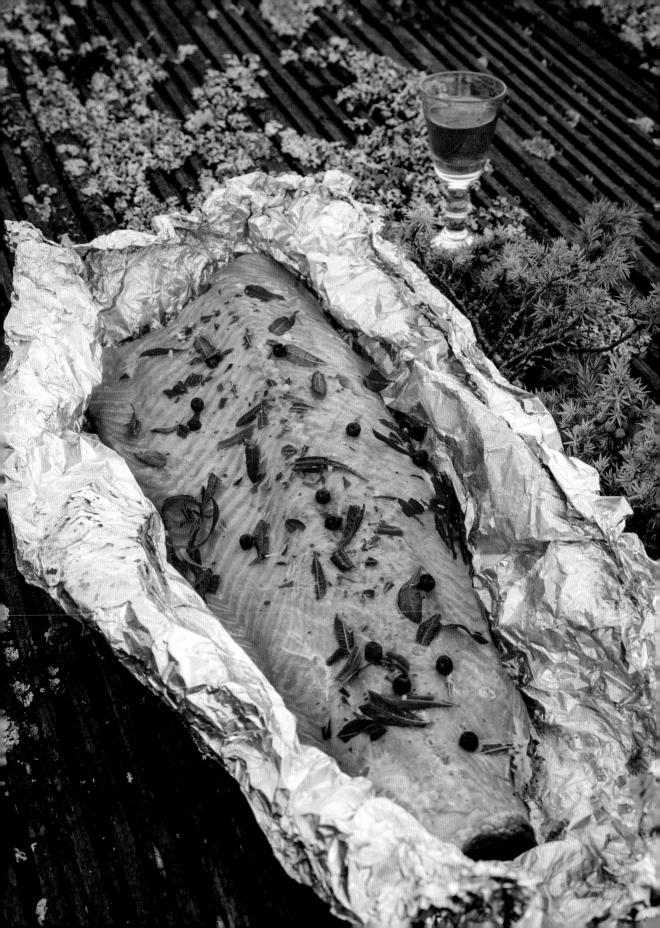

Arisaig Mussels (Loch Ailort)

I couldn't have chosen a better day to visit Ian MacKinnon of Arisaig Mussels at the slipway on Loch Ailort to join him on his boat. It was a blue-sky day in March, the water was clear and calm, and there was a fresh sprinkling of snow on the mountains. With just a few ducks for company, we cut through the glassy water to reach one of Ian's mussel sites while he told me that it was a few drinks at a wedding on Eigg that had got him into fishing. Prior to that he had been kicked out of university and had a series of unfulfilling jobs in and around Glasgow, where he had grown up; his grandparents had moved to Glasgow from Canna and Eigg to make some money in the shipyards so that they could develop the family croft. Sadly, they lost the croft and only visited the islands for holidays. Those drinks at the wedding were with a skipper who offered him a job on his fishing boat.

'So, on 5 May 1985, I found myself on board the vessel *Tyak-Mor* SS216 in Hayle, Cornwall, and I steamed her with skipper Lachie McLean up the west coast to Eigg and started fishing,' Ian recalls with sheer delight on his face. Fishing had brought him back to his west Highland roots.

Within a couple of years Ian got his own boat, but he soon realised that he didn't have the knowledge or the dedication to meet the constant mental and physical demands of a skipper of a fishing vessel. So he moved to Arisaig in 1990 and carried on fishing for lobsters and velvet and brown crabs and thought he would try some mussel farming on the side. He set up an experimental line to see if he could get any mussel spat (larvae) and was so surprised at the success that he applied to the Crown Estate for a seabed lease in Loch Beag at the head of the Sound of Arisaig. But getting a licence is not easy and takes far too long – many people give up during the process. Three long years later, and with the intervention of the local councillor, Ian got a lease for three 50-metre lines, which he installed in 1995 and got his first harvest in 1997. Now he has four sites in Loch Ailort.

Rope-grown mussels are farmed on a three-year cycle, Ian explained as we stopped the boat to pull up some lines. Each year he drops a line to collect spat and each year the line from the previous year matures until the third year when he harvests. This was clear to see in the lines he hauled onto the side of the boat – some were mature and ready to eat while others were the size of a child's fingernail or even smaller.

And so began a fascinating lesson on the processes of mussel farming using 5–10-metre rope droppers, attached to headline ropes, themselves supported by buoys on the surface of the water. The free-floating mussel spat settle on the rope droppers, attaching by their beards, or byssus, and grow.

'When a rope is ready for harvest it's like a 5-metre-long bunch of grapes!' Ian laughed.

In order to harvest that massive 'bunch of grapes', Ian has learnt to use 4–5 metre droppers – any deeper than that and he is competing with other creatures, such as starfish which will attach themselves to the ropes and eat their way up. He also has to keep an eye on the eider ducks, which swim alongside and eat the mussels, knocking many of them off the ropes at the same time.

Ian pointed out the other filter feeders that attach themselves to the droppers – peacock fan worms, which open up under water into delicate fans but close and resemble thick strands of sea spaghetti when you bring them on board, and sea squirts, which look like hollow plastic capsules and when you squeeze them squirt out seawater. There are also the white tube worms and barnacles that attach themselves to the mussel shells – the tube worms are difficult to get rid of but if you leave the barnacles on until October, they will drop off by themselves in November and December. The modern buyer is so discerning that mussels need to be smooth-shelled and barnacle-free to fetch a good price.

The final hazard for Ian is a potential plankton bloom, which takes place in the summer months, creating toxins and removing all the feed out of the water. All of Ian's sites are A-classified and tested regularly for toxins.

He may not be able to compete with the big boys up in Shetland but farming mussels in the west Highlands is an enjoyable way of life. 'It's like planting tatties on a croft,' Ian concludes, with a big, bearded grin. 'You put in the droppers and two years later you pull them out and thank the Good Lord for all you get. Like all fishing!'

Smoked Arisaig Mussel Pâté

The peat-smoked Arisaig Mussels (p.39) from Andy Race Fish Merchants (p.42) give this pâté a unique taste. Creamy and garlicky with an earthy, smoky hit, it is delicious served on toasted bread or oatcakes.

————

Using a blender, blitz the mussels with the garlic. Add the soured cream, ricotta and lemon juice and blitz again. Beat in the parsley and season to taste.

Tip the pâté into a bowl and dust with cayenne or paprika. Serve with toasted bread.

Makes enough for 4 to enjoy as a nibble on toasted bread

————

200g smoked mussels

2 plump garlic cloves, crushed

100g soured cream

100g ricotta

juice of 1 lemon

a small bunch of parsley, finely chopped

sea salt and freshly ground black pepper

cayenne pepper or smoked paprika, for dusting

toasted bread, cut into squares or triangles

Deep-fried Mussels in Beer Batter with Garlicky Walnut Sauce

Choose a local beer for your mussels if you can, such as one from Fyne Ales, Windswept Brewery or Black Isle Brewery – there are a number to choose from. Simply push the golden, crispy-coated, juicy mussels onto sticks and serve them with this walnut sauce or with skordalia (p.144) as a nibble with a drink or as your main dish with a salad.

————

To make the batter, sift the flour, bicarbonate of soda and salt into a bowl. Make a well in the middle and drop in the egg yolks. Gradually pour in the beer, using a wooden spoon to draw in the flour from the sides. Beat well until thick and smooth. Put aside for 30 minutes.

Meanwhile make the walnut sauce. Using a mortar and pestle, pound the walnuts to a paste, or whizz them in an electric blender. Add the bread and garlic, and pound to a paste. Drizzle in the olive oil, stirring all the time, and beat in the lemon juice and honey. Add a dash of vinegar, stir in the parsley and season well with salt and pepper (the sauce should be creamy, so add more olive oil or a little water if it is too thick). Spoon the sauce into a serving bowl.

Serves 4 as a main dish

————

100g plain flour

½ tsp bicarbonate of soda

1 tsp sea salt

2 egg yolks

150ml light beer

roughly 30 fresh, shelled mussels, thoroughly cleaned

sunflower oil, for deep-frying

100g walnuts

2 small slices day-old white bread, with crusts removed, soaked in a little water, and squeezed dry

2 garlic cloves, crushed

3 tbsp olive oil

juice of 1 lemon

1 tsp runny honey

a dash of white wine vinegar

a small bunch of flat-leaf parsley, finely chopped

sea salt and freshly ground black pepper

8 small skewers – 2 skewers per person

Heat enough oil in a shallow pan, or in a wok, for deep-frying. Using your fingers, dip each mussel into the batter and drop them into the oil. Fry them in batches until golden brown and drain on kitchen paper.

Thread the mussels onto small wooden skewers and serve immediately with the walnut sauce for dipping.

Andy Race Fish Merchants

The view to Eigg and Rum was stunning as I drove the stretch of road between Arisaig and Mallaig. The sky was blue, the sun was shining and the islands were white under a fresh dusting of snow, which doesn't happen often on the west coast. Andy Race had nipped home to put the fire on when I arrived at his smokehouse. This gave me time to have a quick browse at the fish counter – small monkfish tails called 'key rings' or 'frogs' by the locals and fishermen, fresh and smoked haddock, hot-smoked salmon, smoked mackerel, smoked langoustines, smoked mussels and the Mallaig kippers which featured in the Channel 4 series *Coastal Railways*, in which Andy showed Julie Walters how to gut and smoke the herring in between their laughter. Afterwards, they sat on the pier eating kippers, smoked salmon and prawns, reminiscing about life.

My eyes also rested on the packets of cold-smoked salmon, which Andy has become renowned for as he selects healthy, sustainably farmed salmon, cures the sides with salt for three to four hours and then cold-smokes over peat and oak for three days, or 'until it's ready', says Andy, who relies on his years of experience to know when it looks and feels right. The 'muscled texture' and robust, smoky taste received an enthusiastic thumbs-up from *The Observer*'s food critic Jay Rayner.

Andy first came to Mallaig in 1979, just as the importance of the busy herring port was coming to an end, and started selling white fish from a van. There were about 100 boats fishing out of Mallaig at that time and there used to be a lively fish market every Tuesday and Thursday evening, including a market just for prawn tails, which would go to scampi factories. Initially, Andy would buy the white

Opposite. Fishing boats and yachts moored at Mallaig, with Eigg and Rum in the distance.

A bold thief!

fish and deliver all over Ardnamurchan and around Fort William in an ordinary van with a set of kitchen scales. He gained most of his fish-merchant knowledge from other ports where he watched people gutting and filleting.

In 1990, Andy set up on his own in a disused Highlands and Islands Council building which he extended and raised to the council's standards. At first there were two shifts, starting with the filleting of the fish bought at the market, from 10 p.m. to 7 a.m. and then the day shift would come in to skin and pack. The fashion at the time was to use a yellow dye for the smoked haddock and a brown one for the kippers, but Andy used the dye just once and got into a messy state with the dye all over his fingers, clothes and the smokehouse floor so decided to leave the fish to take on its natural colour in his two kilns. Then, ironically, he was accused of dying it! Never again would he use dye.

Smoking shellfish 'sort of happened by accident', he says. He simply experimented by putting some langoustines into the smoker one day and was surprised at how good they tasted. Now he smokes oysters, scallops and mussels, as well as langoustines and almost any fish, to order. It was the smoked langoustines I was keen to try, but I couldn't resist the mussels as they come from Ian MacKinnon of Arisaig Mussels (p.39). Both were deliciously juicy with a peat-smoke aroma and flavour. All of Andy's products are available by mail order. Aside from the modern-day restrictions and costs of the packaging, Andy feels that mail order is the way to go.

Bulgur with Smoked Langoustines, Chorizo and Preserved Lemon

When I tasted Andy's smoked langoustines I decided to add them to this Moroccan-inspired dish as they are robust and juicy and work well with other strong flavours. You will need the biggest pan you've got so, if you have a paella pan, use it, otherwise divide the mixture between two frying pans as this is the kind of dish to prepare for a group. It's up to you whether you add the langoustines in their shell or not. I prefer them shelled in this dish and would happily add the smoked Arisaig Mussels shelled too.

Rinse and drain the bulgur. Tip it into a bowl and pour in enough boiling water to cover it. Leave it to absorb the water for 10–15 minutes.

Heat the ghee, or oil, in a large, heavy-based paella pan. Stir in the spices for a minute, then toss in the garlic and jaggery. Add the onion and peppers and sauté for 2–3 minutes to soften. Toss in the chorizo to lightly brown.

Stir in the harissa and the tomato paste, making sure everything is thoroughly mixed. Quickly toss in the bulgur, coating the grains in the tomato mixture, and add the wine. Keep tossing to ensure everything is well mixed together and add more harissa or tomato paste, if you like.

Toss in the smoked langoustines and most of the preserved lemon. Season well to taste and toss in most of the herbs. Garnish with the rest of the preserved lemon and herbs, and serve with a dollop of creamy yoghurt and pickles or chutney.

Serves 6

———

450g coarse bulgur

2 tbsp ghee or rapeseed oil

2 tsp cumin seeds

2 tsp coriander seeds

2 tsp fennel seeds

4–6 garlic cloves, finely chopped

2 tsp jaggery, muscovado sugar or honey

2 onions, finely sliced

2 bell peppers, deseeded and finely sliced

250g mild or hot chorizo, sliced

2 tsp harissa paste

2–3 tbsp tomato paste

250ml white wine

450g smoked langoustines, shelled

rind of 1 preserved lemon, quartered and very finely sliced (reserve some for garnishing)

sea salt and freshly ground black pepper

a bunch of fresh flat-leaf parsley, finely chopped (reserve some for garnishing)

a bunch of fresh coriander, finely chopped (reserve some for garnishing)

Akuri with Smoked Salmon

Akuri is a lightly spiced scrambled egg originating from Persian cuisine but which travelled to India where it is often served for break-fast or as a snack. Add a little smoked salmon, or smoked trout, or even flakes of Mallaig kipper and serve it on buttered toast with a dollop of chutney, pickle or sauce of your choice. This is an ideal way to enjoy offcuts from the highly acclaimed smoked salmon from Andy Race Fish Merchants (p.42). Add a few fine slices to your plate too.

Serves 2

———

6–8 eggs

sea salt and freshly ground black pepper

1 tbsp butter or olive oil

1–2 green chillies, seeded and finely chopped

1 red onion, finely chopped

1 large tomato, seeded and finely chopped

1 tbsp ground turmeric

1 tsp garam masala

a handful of fresh coriander, finely chopped

2–3 slices smoked salmon, cut into thin strips

Beat the eggs lightly with a fork in a bowl and season with salt and pepper.

Melt the butter in a heavy-based pan and stir in the chillies and onion for 2 minutes, add the chopped tomato and stir in the turmeric, garam masala and most of the coriander. Toss in the salmon, then tip in the eggs and stir gently one way and then the other a few times until they begin to scramble.

Pile the scrambled egg onto buttered toast, sprinkle with the rest of the coriander and serve with chutney.

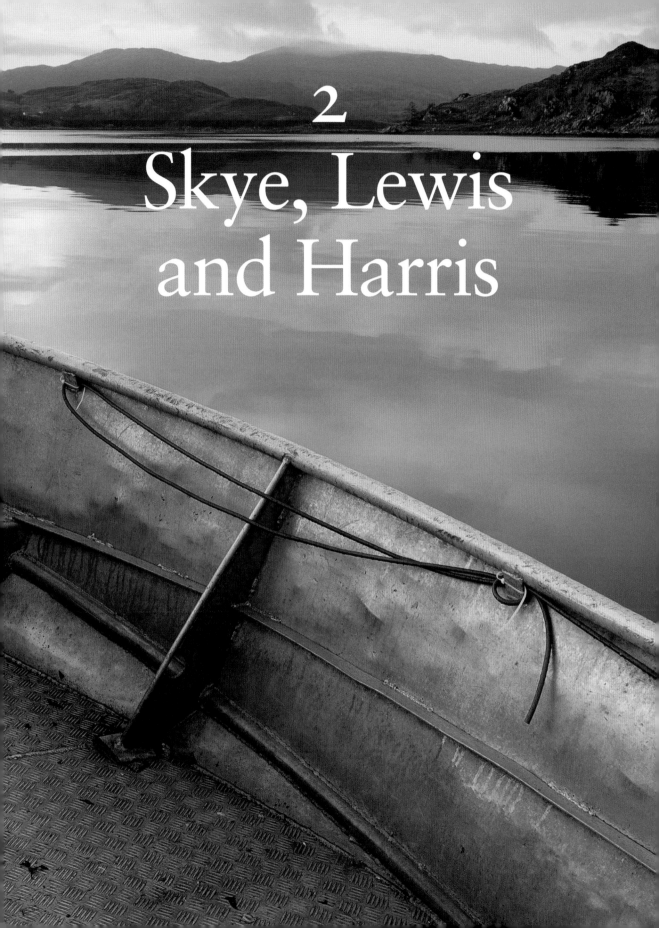

2
Skye, Lewis and Harris

The Isle of Skye lures in visitors for many reasons but, for me, it is Scotland's 'shellfish capital', not just because of the quantity and quality of prawns and scallops landed there but also because some of the best seafood chefs are based on the island. The shellfish industry on Skye – farmed, dived and creeled – has taken over from the once-prominent herring industry when Portree harbour was packed with fishing boats. A ferry ride over to Lewis, Harris and the Uists transports you to white beaches, seafood shacks, smokehouses and sugar-kelp harvesting. During the herring boom, Stornoway, meaning 'anchor bay', was regarded as a major port strategically positioned facing the ports of Kyle of Lochalsh and Mallaig on the mainland.

Isle of Skye Sea Salt

The stunning Isle of Skye has some of the best shellfish in the world and some of the best chefs to cook it too. It is also home to the most delicious and beautifully packaged sea salt, a product that hadn't been produced on Skye for 300 years until Chris and Meena Watts decided to give it a go. I crossed the iconic Skye Bridge on a bright autumn day, and after an hour's drive north towards Uig, I turned off the main road onto a single-track to meet the salt's creators. Meena jumped into my car and we followed Chris along a dirt track through grassy croft land from where you can spot the tops of the polytunnels right by the shore. As Meena chatted excitedly about their salt production journey, I got the sense that they relished the freedom of being out on their own in a remote and peaceful location on Loch Snizort in the north of Skye, deeply proud to be creating something so natural and special.

It had been a light-bulb moment for Chris one day when he was standing at the kitchen window of the eco house they had built on Skye. All the natural ingredients were there – sun, wind, and the chance to build a business based on one of the island's traditional resources, the sea. He researched salt production and was drawn to the solar evaporation method of hot countries rather than the vacuum distillation taking place in the UK. But then they would need to make it work in a northern latitude! He and Meena were no strangers to going with the flow and making projects come to life through innovative thinking and hard work. Before coming to live on Skye, they had managed over 90 VSO projects on sustainability in Papua New Guinea, Chris had been involved in urban regeneration projects across the UK through his co-founded sustainability consultancy Beyond Green, and Meena had worked on sustainable projects in places like Latvia, South Africa, Argentina and India, as well as managing the setting up of the Health Promotion infrastructure in Estonia, for which she won an international award. Becoming the pioneers of modern salt production in polytunnels in Scotland was well within their realms of possibility. After two years of trials, they had developed a solar evaporation process using ponds inside polytunnels. Isle of Skye Sea Salt was first produced in 2013.

Chris and Meena rented land from a wonderful local crofter family who helped to clear and level it. The spoil was piled up between the four polytunnels and the shore to create a natural wind-break which, combined with Paraweb attached to a fence, reduces the wind speed by as much as 60 per cent, protecting the tunnels from winter storms that sweep up the loch. Three of the polytunnels are the 'ponds' into which the water is pumped at high tide. It takes one and half hours to fill the base of these 'ponds' where water is left to evaporate under the heat of the sun while the wind blows through the tunnels to reduce the moisture so that natural salt crystals form. The whole process is rather magical and, as the light changes, casting shadows and reflections within these 'pond' structures, you feel as if you could be walking through the arches of classical Roman columns.

Between April and September there are four harvests of approximately 600 kilos of crystals which are collected while they are still damp and laid out in the fourth polytunnel, the 'drying tunnel', to allow any excess moisture to drip off before the final stage of the drying process in a dehydrator. Salt is naturally antibacterial so there aren't any risks in its production and the resulting mineral-rich crystals are clean, crisp and chunky with a hint of soft sweetness on the tongue – perfect rubbed or sprinkled over the fish and shellfish that Skye is renowned for, or you could copy Chris and stir a little into your coffee.

Meena and Chris have loved creating sea salt on Skye, their home, where they are part of many community-related events. From loch to larder, unrefined and packed with minerals, the salt is quite simply as pure and sustainable as it could possibly be and that is important to Chris and Meena who believe in working in harmony with nature. The same ethos has gone into the carefully designed packaging in eco-friendly boxes with a contemporary Scottish design and the salt keeps winning the top awards. By kick-starting the dormant sea salt industry in Scotland, they have become an inspiration and catalyst for other salt producers both here and abroad. In fact, OpitoBay Salt Company, a salt producer in New Zealand, has named its polytunnels Chris and Meena after these two passionate pioneers!

Smoked Mackerel Pâté
with Isle of Skye Sea Salt Za'atar

Classic, lemony, smoked mackerel pâté is quick and easy to make, and delicious as a starter, a light lunch with a salad or a nibble with drinks. I like to serve it generously dolloped – you just can't be skimpy with it – on toasted bread, chunks of fresh crusty baguette, snappy crackers or homemade oatcakes (see p.176 for the recipe) and then generously sprinkled – again don't skimp – with freshly made za'atar. The fresh, zingy Isle of Skye Sea Salt is perfect for this toasted-tasting, thyme-driven spice mix which lifts the smooth pâté with its crystal crunch.

Remove the skin and any bones from the mackerel fillets and break them up into a blender. Add the cream cheese, creamed horseradish, lemon juice and a good grinding of black pepper and blend until smooth. Taste the pâté to see if you need more lemon – sometimes you do if the fruit aren't very juicy. Tip the pâté into a bowl.

In a small pan, dry roast the sesame seeds until they begin to colour. Toss in the thyme and sumac and keep tossing for a minute until fragrant. Toss in the salt and tip the mixture into a bowl.

If serving the pâté in a bowl, drizzle a little olive oil over the top and sprinkle with some of the za'atar. Tip the rest of za'atar into another bowl for people to help themselves. If serving the pâté in individual portions make sure each one has a good coating of za'atar, and if serving the pâté as a canapé on oatcakes, spoon or sprinkle za'atar on top of each one. The key is no skimping!

Serves 4–6 as a starter or roughly 24 canapé oatcakes

For the pâté

200–300g moist, plump, hot-smoked mackerel fillets

250g Philadelphia cream cheese

1 heaped tsp creamed horseradish

juice of 2 lemons

freshly ground black pepper

For the za'atar

2 tbsp sesame seeds

2 tbsp dried thyme

1 tbsp sumac

1–2 tsp Isle of Skye Sea Salt

Dry Prawn and Potato Curry

Serves 3–4

_____

For the spice paste

4 garlic cloves, peeled and chopped

25g fresh ginger, peeled and chopped

2 red chillies, stalks and seeds removed, and chopped

1 tsp Isle of Skye Sea Salt

1 tsp ground turmeric

1 tbsp mild or hot curry powder, depending on how much heat you like

_____

2 tbsp ghee, or vegetable oil with a little butter

1 onion, peeled, cut in half lengthways, and sliced along the grain

a handful of fresh or dried curry leaves

1 cinnamon stick

2–3 large waxy potatoes, lightly steamed, peeled and diced

500g fresh large prawns, shelled and deveined

300ml coconut milk

Isle of Skye Sea Salt

2 tsp fennel seeds

2 tsp brown mustard seeds

a small bunch of fresh coriander, roughly chopped

In Scotland, we are a nation of curry eaters – in Glasgow it could be considered the 'national' dish – but we often think of a curry as a hot, spicy and saucy dish. In India, Pakistan, Bangladesh and amongst the Indian communities in East Africa where I grew up, curries are often fragrant rather than hot and they are regarded as 'dry' or 'wet'. A 'dry' curry simply indicates that there is very little liquid in the finished dish, which lends itself to being scooped up easily with flat-breads. This recipe calls for pre-cooked potatoes, which can either be of an ordinary waxy variety, or a sweet potato. If you want to stick with tradition, this curry would be served with flatbreads, a yoghurt dish and chutney. This one is for Meena from Isle of Skye Sea Salt!

_____

Using a mortar and pestle, pound the garlic, ginger and chillies with the salt to a coarse paste. Stir in the turmeric and curry powder.

Heat the ghee in a heavy-based pan or an earthenware pot. Stir in the onion and fry until golden. Add the curry leaves, followed by the cinnamon stick and the spice paste. Fry the paste until fragrant, then add the potatoes, coating them in the spices. Toss in the prawns and cook for 1–2 minutes. Stir in the coconut milk and bubble it up to thicken and reduce. Season to taste with salt.

Quickly, toast the fennel and mustard seeds in a small heavy-based pan, until they begin to pop and give off a nutty aroma. Stir them into the curry, sprinkle coriander over the top and serve with flat-breads, yoghurt and chutney.

Michael Smith, Chef Patron of Loch Bay

_____

As I drove along the narrow coastal road, the calm sea looking inviting in the warm sunshine, with the whitewashed Stein Inn and row of terraced houses on one side and neat private gardens with hydrangeas and yuccas on the other, and the sound of Italian opera flowing through the windows, I felt I should have been on a scooter heading to my favourite trattoria. But I was on the Isle of Skye, parking outside the Michelin-starred restaurant, Loch Bay.

The heads of a wee Jack Russell and a handsome man popped out of one of the upstairs windows. 'You're early,' he said. 'I'll be down in a minute.'

Well, of course I was early. I had come to see Michael Smith, whose reputation reaches far beyond the shores of Skye and whose restaurant, which is booked months in advance, is located on a remote sea loch in the north of the island, where there is very little signage to guide you there. I had left in plenty of time.

'People pay in full when they book, so they will find it,' Michael reasons with a cheeky grin.

Loch Bay is unapologetically all about local shellfish, the freshest and the best there is. The discreet restaurant, which is also where Michael and his family live, is right by the jetty where the boat takes passengers to St Kilda and where local creel fisherman Iain Matheson of Loch Bay Shellfish steps off his boat and passes his catch through the kitchen window. About 20 fresh lobsters were already sitting in the sink when Michael took me through to his kitchen. The menu is entitled 'Skye Fruits de Mer' and takes you through a five-course *dégustation*. Loch to pan to plate – you just can't get fresher than that. The proteins are the star ingredients and the rest is dictated by seasonality and availability. Michael instinctively knows how to create the best flavours possible using what is available on the island. Less is more: the food should speak for itself and the fresh flavours should sing.

Michael started working in a restaurant in Inverness when he was 15 and loved the energy of the kitchen. In the early 1990s he spread his wings and found work in the top French restaurants in London, including Le Gavroche and Le Pont de la Tour, becoming senior sous chef at the Blueprint Café under Jeremy Lee. To this day he credits Jeremy with his approach to ingredients and menu selection. Back in Scotland, he developed the kitchens and menus for several new restaurants in Glasgow. There he met Shirley Spear, who asked him to take over The Three Chimneys in 2004. Seizing the opportunity, as well as a good lifestyle choice for his young family, Michael moved to Skye and remained at The Three Chimneys for 11 years, gaining it a Michelin star in 2014 and the reputation of 'one of the top 50 destinations in the world'.

Michael set up Loch Bay in 2016 and was awarded a Michelin star within 18 months. He can seat a maximum of 18, in two sittings, to keep service manageable for his small team of dedicated staff – Graeme, Issy and Bren. His lovely French wife, Laurence, who he met in his London days at Le Pont de la Tour, is front of house. So, Loch Bay really is a family affair, offering the ultimate Skye shellfish experience and bringing together the contemporary Scottish- and French-influenced narrative of the owners.

Loch Bay Prawns with Tarragon Beurre Blanc

Michael chose this dish for inclusion in the book as it reflects the marriage of classic French gastronomy with the freshest local crustaceans of Skye. It is his take on the classic Pot-au-feu. In the restaurant, he represents the 'stew' components by serving the prawns tossed in a tarragon-flavoured beurre blanc on a bed of hot carrot purée, with crispy potatoes in Cabernet Sauvignon vinegar, gem lettuce hearts and pickled cucumber. To finish the dish one whole prawn is split open, glazed with the beurre blanc and popped under the grill. So, here we have the recipe for the peeled prawns dressed in the sweet, velvety, piquant butter sauce.

• • •

Langoustines, or Dublin Bay prawns, are just called 'prawns' on Skye. You can source fresh live prawns from some fishermen and fishmongers. They don't need to be large – in fact the smaller ones are more succulent and sweet. Put the live prawns in the freezer, or at a temperature of −1°C for half an hour to stun them so that they go into a state of hibernation before cooking.

Serves 2

————

For the beurre blanc

several stalks of fresh tarragon

150ml best-quality white wine vinegar

½ banana shallot, finely sliced

a pinch of Isle of Skye Sea Salt

50ml double cream

150g unsalted butter, diced and kept chilled in the fridge

————

roughly 12 fresh, medium-sized, live prawns, kept at −1°C to stun them into hibernation before cooking

chopped chervil, celery leaves or parsley, for garnishing

————

To make the beurre blanc, first pick off the tarragon leaves, chop them finely and put aside for later. Chop the stalks and pop them into a small pot with the vinegar, sliced shallot and the sea salt. Place the pot over a moderate heat and reduce the vinegar by two-thirds.

Strain the vinegar reduction and return to the pot. Stir in the cream and bring to the boil. Reduce the heat and simmer for 3–4 minutes until it thickens.

Take the pot off the heat and gradually add in the diced butter, using a micro whisk if you have one, or a wooden spoon, allowing the butter to melt and be incorporated so that you end up with a thick, shiny sauce. (Be patient as this stage, adding the butter bit by bit, otherwise the sauce will split.) Taste the sauce to check the seasoning and acidity – it should leave the 'inside of your cheeks salivating' – perhaps it needs another pinch of salt or a squeeze of lemon juice to achieve the right piquancy. Once you are happy with it, stir in the chopped tarragon leaves. Keep the sauce in a warm environment while you prepare the prawns.

Bring a large pot of heavily salted water to a rolling boil and drop in the prawns for 3–4 minutes. Lift them out of the pot and plunge them straight into iced water. Keep two whole prawns for garnishing and peel the rest (don't throw away the shells as they can be used for a stock or bisque later).

To split the two whole prawns in half for garnishing, take one and place it on a board, stretch it out with its back facing up, then insert the sharp point of a knife halfway along the body and slice down towards the head, turn the prawn 180 degrees and slice down to the tail so that you have two perfect prawn halves. Repeat the process with the second whole prawn.

Using a pastry brush, or the back of a teaspoon, glaze the halved prawns with a layer of the tarragon butter and pop them under a hot grill for 1–2 minutes to lightly brown. Toss the rest of the prawns in the tarragon butter and pile them in individual serving dishes. Place the two glazed halves on top and garnish with a little chervil, young celery leaves or parsley.

• • •

Alternatively, you could split all the prawns in half lengthways, place them on a baking tray, glaze them with the tarragon butter and place them under the hot grill for 1–2 minutes, until nicely browned.

Just Hooked (Portree)

We serve all types of customer here, from my old stagiaire company Barrufet who still buy daily for the Barcelona market, or the Michelin-starred or aspiring restaurant doing their very best to present the island's produce in the most tastebud-tantalising way, to the household cook on a budget, so we have to consider all types of produce from the luxurious Minch scallop to locally farmed mussels or salmon.

The road from Uig, the small fishing village in the north of Skye where Mairi Evans grew up, to the premises of Just Hooked, the award-winning fishmonger in Portree, is a short one compared to the journey she has been on to get there. Like Calum Montgomery (p.63), who is one of Just Hooked's loyal customers, Mairi was raised on Skye, went to the mainland to study and work, but came back because she loves it. And she loves working with fish, the fishing industry and all the people associated with it. She says she may have inherited her 'fishing' gene from her great-grandmother who was a herring girl in Uig at a time when the women of the Hebrides formed the backbone of the fishing industry.

After studying export marketing and languages in Edinburgh, Mairi's journey began with Barrufet SA, one of the main wholesalers in the commercial fish market in Mercabarna, Barcelona, where she gained experience with fish from all over the world. Her next stop was Stornoway, where she worked with the local council, Comhairle nan Eilean Siar, and Highlands and Islands Enterprise to deliver an EU-funded initiative to diversify markets for fishing and fish farming in the Western Isles and which gave her an insight into Scotland's fishing industry. From Stornoway, Mairi went to Aberdeen to work as a seafood trader for Salmac to help diversify their established salmon product base to shellfish and other species. One of the things she loved about that job was the early morning trip up to the Peterhead fish auctions to select the best for the company's customers in Glasgow, London, Spain and beyond. Still in Aberdeen, Mairi was recruited to set up a sales division for a partnership between two Norwegian companies that were running salmon farms off Shetland.

With this huge breadth of knowledge right across the fishing industry, Mairi returned to Skye with her husband-to-be, Lee, and set up Just Hooked as an export trading company for seafood. Now 20 years in business, the team at Just Hooked shares the ethos to source as responsibly as possible and to promote local produce in order to serve the community, whilst maintaining contacts with their export customers. As the local fishing trade is dying, this means sourcing from the Western Isles, up and down the west coast and at the auctions in Kinlochbervie, Scrabster, Fraserburgh and Peterhead to offer a regular and varied choice, such as halibut, sea trout, sea bass, haddock, salmon, langoustines, crabs, lobsters and scallops.

Calum Montgomery

Born and bred on the Isle of Skye and chef patron of Edinbane Lodge, Calum Montgomery is as rooted in the local *terroir* as his ingredients. Yet he doesn't like to use the word 'local' for the produce on his menu as he feels it is overused and misused; instead he tells you in detail where every ingredient comes from. All the seafood used to be delivered to his door by his wife's late uncle, Neillie 'Beag' MacInnes from Luib, but now he sources it from other family members and friends: scallops from James Cameron of Skye Scallop Divers (p.68); mussels from his cousin, Peter Macaskill of Drumfearn; langoustines, crabs and Skye shrimps from Iain Matheson of Loch Bay Shellfish; lobsters straight off the boats or from Just Hooked (p.62); and halibut, hake, turbot and monkfish from his uncle's boat, *Asteria*. Aside from shellfish, the only seafood that the Skye fishermen are allowed to land regularly are octopus, monkfish, conger eel and line-caught mackerel.

The village of Edinbane lies just off the road to Dunvegan in the north of Skye and is one of historic significance, as the first hospital on the island was built there. It also where Edinbane Lodge, an inn dating back to 1543 and reputed to be the oldest building of hospitality on Skye, is situated. When Calum and his family bought it in 2017 it was run down and dirty, but with all hands on deck, they

spent nine months stripping back plasterboard, lifting up floors, and painting and decorating to restore it to its former glory, before opening it once again as a building of hospitality, a restaurant with rooms. Their first overnight guest just happened to be an inspector and he was so delighted with his stay he gave them five stars for the rooms and three rosettes for the restaurant.

The star of the show, though, is the menu, which is dictated daily by Calum's suppliers, showcasing the seasonality and provenance of Skye's best produce while it is still on the island – roughly 98 per cent of the shellfish leaves the island in trucks to go to places like London, France, Spain and China. Calum is convinced that the seafood on Skye is amongst the best in the world, if not the best. When menu items are not from Skye, their source is always noted, such as the cod from Shetland, and, because there isn't a dairy on Skye, the butter from Orkney and the cheddar from Mull.

Calum's passion for cooking began at the age of 14 when he took on a kitchen porter job at the Cuillin Hills Hotel in Portree. This led to chef training at the City of Glasgow College with chef lecturer Gary Maclean (p.ix), a role model for Calum, at the helm. Calum's next steps were work experience placements at One Devonshire Gardens in Glasgow and at Kinloch Lodge (p.70) in the south of Skye where, at 23 years old, he found himself promoted to sous chef in a Michelin-starred restaurant. He also represented Scotland on the BBC TV series *Great British Menu*. For Calum and his team, the mantra is fresh, clean, simple and no rush. He only opens four days a week for 30 covers so that guests can take their time to enjoy his creative and textured menu, 'Taste of Skye', one of the many reasons why Edinbane Lodge won Restaurant of the Year 2023 at the Scottish Excellence Awards.

Edinbane Baked Oysters with
Brown Crab and Pepper Dulse Butter

Serves 4 (2 oysters each)

———

200g Orkney butter

5g rehydrated dried pepper dulse, chopped

8 Pacific oysters

200g picked crab claw meat

50g toasted panko breadcrumbs

pepper dulse powder

When Calum first tasted this dish in New Orleans, he was blown away by the flavour combination but was convinced it would taste even better with fresh oysters and crab from Skye. He first tried it out at the musical festival Skye Live and ended up preparing 600 of these stuffed oysters in one evening. It is now a regular item on his Edinbane menu.

Place the Orkney butter on a high heat until a 'beurre noisette' – the butter turning brown but not burnt – is achieved. Remove from the heat, stir in the chopped pepper dulse and leave to infuse for 1 hour.

Meanwhile, preheat the oven to 230°C (fan 210°C), 450°F, gas mark 8.

Using a hand blender, pulse the beurre noisette and pepper dulse until smooth.

Shuck the oysters, discard the liquid and dry the oysters on a kitchen cloth. Place them back in the shells and top each one with 25g crabmeat. Spoon the infused butter over the top, place the shells on an oven tray and pop them in the oven for 3 minutes.

Remove from the oven and top with the breadcrumbs followed by a light dusting of pepper dulse powder. Serve immediately and, if you are by the coast, you might like to garnish the oysters with arrowgrass or sea plantain.

A Day in the Life of Skye Scallop Divers

James Cameron worked as a commercial diver in Aberdeen and Iceland, where he met his wife, and then moved to Skye where he started diving for scallops out of Tayvallich, near Oban, learning the skills on week-long trips around Islay, Jura, Tiree and Colonsay. After two years he had saved enough money to buy his own boat, along with his friend Alberto Morales, and they set up Skye Scallop Divers. The boat, *Concord* KY99, was a 28-foot prawn trawler that they converted into a vessel for gathering hand-dived scallops, which they sell to the local market, delivering to Calum Montgomery (p.63) and other chefs and restaurants around Skye; they also supply Andy Richardson's 'Scallop Express' (p.206) destined for David Lowrie Fish Merchants (p.203) in Fife, on the east coast.

For Skye Scallop Divers, the day starts early, around 4 a.m. or 5 a.m., when James and his crew set off from Staffin, where they live, and board *Concord* KY99 around 5 a.m. or 6 a.m. in Kyleakin. They then set off to the scallop grounds, which are determined by the weather but usually they steam for two or three hours to their destination. In winter, the aim is to reach the grounds by first light. This can be a rough, stormy journey or a magical one with the sun rising and dolphins accompanying the boat. Whilst heading out, James and his crew fill their diving cylinders with the onboard compressor and have a coffee and a chat about where they will dive, studying the charts and repairing net bags for the scallops.

When they arrive at the grounds, one diver gets into the water with a large bag which has a rope attached to it with a buoy to mark his location. The two divers left on board just wait and watch. They need to keep an eye on the buoy and the diver's bubbles to make sure he is OK. A dive can last between one to two hours, depending on the depth; if decompression is needed on the way up, the diver has to wait at around three metres' depth to get the accumulated nitrogen out of his system otherwise he would suffer from the bends. When the diver pops up to the surface, James steams the boat over, drops the ladder so the diver can climb on board, puts the buoy and rope into the hauler to pull the bag of scallops to the surface and empty it into the boat, and the next diver drops into the water. While the second diver is in the water, the first diver sorts his scallops by

size and bags them up in net sacks for storage on the seabed at the end of the day.

The Skye Scallop Divers' boat in Kyleakin.

The team of three usually dive three times a day and then they steam back to the harbour when they lose the light. This can mean arriving in Kyleakin as late as 8 p.m. or 9 p.m. and, once they have put the net bags of scallops in a line on a rope and dropped them back in the sea to keep them alive and fresh, they head home for around 11 p.m. with deliveries to restaurants on the way. It is a long day.

James and crew believe that scallop diving is the most environmentally friendly way of fishing but, in order to keep the fishery sustainable, he moves the boat around the Isle of Skye and also goes further afield, up and down the west coast on week-long trips, sleeping on the boat. This gives the scallop grounds plenty of chance to recover. By the time he and the crew have circled the island most spots have replenished themselves with good-sized clams. Skye Scallop Divers has one goal and that is to maintain high-value, low-volume fishery by only catching the best-quality and most-sought-after sizes of scallops and treating them with the utmost care from when they pick them off the seabed until they arrive at whatever restaurant or wholesaler they are going to.

Jordan's Cod Brandade at Kinloch Lodge

Serves 4, as a dip

For the cure

500g cod fish trim, or cod fillets

50g sea salt

20g demerara sugar

1 tsp smoked paprika

zest and juice of 1 lemon

2 tbsp olive oil

1 medium onion, chopped

1 stick celery, chopped

2 garlic cloves, chopped

3 basil stalks

roughly 600ml milk

100g softened butter

1 tbsp horseradish cream

1 tbsp chopped capers

juice of ½ lime

sea salt and freshly ground black pepper

As you cross a stretch of peaty moorland on the road to Sleat in the south of Skye, a white lodge comes into view, set on the shore of Loch na Dal, looking over to Knoydart on the mainland. This is Kinloch Lodge, inherited as a run-down shooting lodge in 1970 by Lord Godfrey Macdonald and his wife, Lady Claire. Both wanted to create a lodge they would like to stay in with food they would enjoy eating, and with Claire's flair for cooking local produce they gradually put Skye on the culinary map. They opened their doors in 1972 to four guests and now their daughter Isabella, with her own charm and vision, opens the doors to thousands from all over the world. The original ethos of genuine Highland hospitality remains and the locally sourced produce is now in the hands of Jordan Webb with his relaxed approach of cooking food that he would like to eat – simple, seasonal, unpretentious.

Jordan joined the team at Kinloch Lodge in 2020 and set about restoring the polytunnel in which they now grow a variety of vegetables for the kitchen, growing herbs in pots around the lodge and foraging for wild produce including seaweed. He brines fish with kelp, makes kombu stocks and dashis to tighten the flesh of the fish and enhance its flavour, and he adds sea coriander, sea aster and sea plantain to dishes. A period as a chef in Australia taught him how to salt and smoke seafood, how to concentrate the flavour by leaving it to breathe and how to use every part. His peat-smoked salmon is delicious as he vacuum seals it with Talisker to penetrate the fish.

Here, he treats us to a salt cure to make cod brandade which can be used in two ways – as a dip and as a fried cake with a langoustine vinaigrette (see p.73 for the recipe).

Place the fish in shallow dish, sprinkle with the salt, sugar, paprika and lemon zest, and squeeze the lemon juice over it. Cover and leave the fish to cure for 48 hours, turning the fish in the brine solution from time to time.

After curing for 48 hours, lift the fish out of brine solution and pat dry. Heat the olive oil in a high-sided pan and fry the onion and celery with the garlic and basil until they have softened, but not

coloured. Place the fish on top of the vegetables in the pan and pour in enough milk to just cover. Bring the milk to a gentle simmer to poach the fish for 10 minutes. Stir the pan occasionally to make sure the milk is not catching.

After the fish has poached, lift it out of the pan and place it on a tray to cool slightly. Discard the milk and vegetables. While still warm, blitz the fish in a food processor (or beat in a bowl) with the butter, horseradish cream and lime juice. Fold in the chopped capers, season to taste and serve with hot buttered toast.

Jordan's Brandade Cakes with Langoustine Vinaigrette

At Kinloch Lodge, Jordan serves his brandade as a dip, but also uses the mixture to make little fish cakes, served with this deliciously fresh langoustine vinaigrette. To make the cakes, just add an egg and roughly 2 tablespoons of breadcrumbs, or plain flour, to the brandade mixture (see p.70) so that you can mould it into little balls – the mixture will make 8 cakes – and then fry them in olive or rapeseed oil until golden brown.

Preheat the oven to 180°C (fan 160°C), 350°F, gas mark 4.

Bring a pot of salted water to the boil with the onion, fennel and lime juice. Drop in the langoustines for 2½ minutes, then drain and refresh in iced cold water. Peel the langoustines and chop into 1cm chunks. Keep aside.

Place the red peppers on a roasting tray, drizzle with olive oil and place in the oven for about 15 minutes, turning once halfway through, until their skins have a brown-roasted colour and are pulling away from the flesh.

Take the peppers out of the oven and place them in a sealable tub with the lid on. This makes the pepper steam out which gives off a lovely juice to collect for the dressing. When cool enough to handle, peel the pepper over the container to collect any further juice. Dice the pepper flesh and tip it into a bowl. Strain the pepper juice and keep for the dressing.

To the diced roast pepper in the bowl, add the diced cucumber, onion, fennel, avocado and parsley. Toss in the lime juice, olive oil and half the strained red pepper juice. Season to taste.

Fry the brandade cakes until golden. When nearly ready to serve mix the diced langoustines through the pepper mix, add the table-spoon of salmon roe and spoon onto plates with the warm brandade cakes.

For the vinaigrette

1kg live langoustines, kept at –1°C to stun them into hibernation before cooking

2–3 slices of onion

2–3 slices of fennel bulb

juice of ½ lime

2 red peppers

½ cucumber, finely diced

½ red onion, finely diced

½ fennel bulb, finely diced

1 ripe avocado, diced

1 tbsp chopped parsley

juice of 2 limes

4 tbsp extra virgin oil

1 tbsp salmon roe

The Skye Ghillie's Foraged Cockle Broth
with Pepper Dulse and Wild Garlic Bulbs

As a child, Mitchell Partridge spent many years in Lossiemouth, on the Moray coast, where he foraged in woodlands and hedgerows with his grandad. He now lives in Carbost, on the Isle of Skye, over-looking Loch Harport. He has built up a reputation for himself as the 'Skye Ghillie' and guides visitors around the island's best spots for stalking, fishing, walking and foraging.

Mitchell can often be spotted around Kinloch Lodge with his collie, also called Ghillie, as he has been taking the lodge guests out for nature and foraging walks for the last 20 years. Classed as a 'leisure fisherman', Mitchell doesn't require a licence to pull up five creels a day, land five crabs or one lobster a day, or to fish for pollock and mackerel. He forages for spoots, urchins, mussels, cockles, clams and seaweed. He is also a Maritime Mammal Medic.

For this deliciously fresh, foraged broth, Mitchell went down to the shore and scraped the surface of the silt and sand with the heel of his boot and filled a pan full of cockles in five minutes. After washing them in a freshwater burn he collected some pepper dulse, the truffle of the sea, which he carefully cut off the holdfast with scissors to limit disturbance. Then he headed to the woods to clear a patch of its leaf litter and gently scraped away the surface of the soil with his fingers to reveal wild garlic bulbs – just small ones but they packed a punch.

Now Mitchell was ready to cook, so he got a small fire going on the beach and simmered his cockles in fresh water from a nearby burn until they just opened allowing the salt water to mix with the fresh, lessening the saltiness of the broth. He then transferred the cockles to the shallower lid of his pot and added a generous knob of unsalted butter along with the pepper dulse and wild garlic bulbs, cooking them just long enough to get a waft of smoke from the fire to add to the flavour and all the time adding some of the cockle stock from the pot. Then it was time to tuck into his delicious wild broth with earth- and smoke-stained fingers!

Before leaving the beach, Mitchell made sure that the leaves and earth in the woods were returned to how he found them, that the

cockle shells were distributed over the sand to be drawn into the sea
and that the fire was dismantled and scattered. The Skye Ghillie
enjoyed his wild dinner but left no trace.

Grilled Spoots with Fino Sherry, Smoked Paprika and Oregano Breadcrumbs

Steamed, stir-fried, grilled, simmered in a broth, cooked in the embers of a fire, spoots, or razor clams, are versatile and delicious. To gather the spoots, you need to look for their round, figure-of-eight holes in the sand and cover them with ordinary salt, which makes them emerge. Carefully grab them by the shell and pull them out.

Serves 2–4

2 slices day-old bread, crumbed

2 tbsp Parmesan, finely grated

2 tsp dried oregano or thyme

olive oil

12 fresh spoots, thoroughly cleaned

roughly 200ml fino sherry

2 garlic cloves, crushed

a scant tsp smoked paprika

sea salt

In a small bowl, mix together the breadcrumbs with the grated Parmesan and oregano and, using your fingertips, rub in enough olive oil to moisten the mixture.

Place the spoots in a pan with the fino sherry over a hot heat for a minute, so that they open. Lift the spoots out of the pan and add 3 tablespoons of olive oil, the garlic and smoked paprika to the sherry. Simmer over a low heat to reduce. Season to taste with the sea salt.

Take the spoot meat out of the shells and remove the small sac. Cut the meat into 2 or 3 pieces and divide them amongst the shells. Place the shells on a grill or oven tray and drizzle the reduced sherry over them. Scatter the breadcrumbs generously over the top and pop under the grill for a minute or two to brown the crumbs. Serve immediately.

Pan-fried Whelks with Bacon

Serves 2–4

8–10 whelks

100g smoked or plain butter

2 garlic cloves, chopped

6–8 smoked streaky bacon rashers, cut into pieces

sea salt and black pepper, or pepper dulse

mustard, Worcestershire sauce, ketchup, chilli sauce, for serving

My son has cooked whelks much more often than I have and he enjoys them. They are not for everyone. You need to rinse them well to rid them of their slime – they are essentially a sea snail – and the gunk they pick up while grazing. But once you've got over the cleaning they can be pan-fried with strong flavours, such as garlic, chorizo, bacon, black pudding, pepper dulse or a splash of whisky. They can be fiddly to get out the shells, but they do make a damned good snack.

Bring a pot of salted water to the boil and tip in the whelks or cockles for 2 minutes. Drain and immediately plunge into cold water. Using a sharpened stick or an escargot fork, pull the meat out of the shells. Remove and discard the discs and sacs and, if the whelks are quite big, chop them into a few pieces.

Melt the butter in a heavy-based pan and stir in the garlic, until it begins to colour. Toss in the bacon for a minute, then add the whelks, until they begin to go crisp at the edges. Season with black pepper or pepper dulse.

Enjoy them on buttered toast, or with eggs, and with a little mustard, ketchup, Worcester sauce or hot sauce of your choice.

Isle of Skye Mussel Company

On the Sleat peninsula of Skye, sitting with Andy Airnes and Jude Brown and their sweet black lab in their static caravan on a plot of rough croft land, their new home under construction a short distance away, I was surprised at how unfazed they seemed by their huge undertaking. And not just the ongoing building and planting of the croft but the acquisition of a dilapidated mussel farm. With not a mussel in sight!

I quickly learned that it was all part of a new adventure, and that Andy and Jude are no strangers to those. They met on Ascension Island, in the middle of the South Atlantic Ocean, where Andy managed Green Mountain National Park, after years of working as a safari guide in Africa and leading overland expeditions in South America, and where Jude managed the conservation and fisheries department and was, in fact, his boss. Jude is a marine biologist with a Masters in Aquaculture and a PhD in fisheries. She has worked as a researcher in Antarctica and South Georgia, in commercial fisheries in the Falklands, in marine diversity in St Helena, in tilapia farming in Kenya and has set up a marine consultancy business. So, for these two, a mussel farm without any mussels doesn't present a major obstacle.

Mussel farming is low impact, they explain. There is no requirement for chemical treatments, use of antibiotics or input of feed. They don't take up any of the limited space left on land and they don't require freshwater in their farming, making them a sustainable animal protein option that could help to provide healthy diets without impacting the planet. With an increasing global population, there is a need for more sustainable food sources that also meet human nutritional needs. 'This should be music to mussel farmers' ears,' Jude says. 'We have the answer hanging in the ocean, we just need to get the message out there!'

The Isle of Skye Mussel Company operates within one of only 13 Grade A shellfish protected waters in the whole of the UK, all of which are found in Scotland, on the west coast and the Northern Isles. Jude explains to me that there are three grades of water quality around the UK – A, B and C. Water quality at food production sites is tested throughout the year and assessed to establish quality grading. Samples have to maintain clarity standards for several years to establish a grade. Food grown and produced in Grade A waters is judged to be fit for human consumption without further processing. For a water area to be classified 'Grade A' and 'shellfish protected', there has to be land and aquatic management at water catchment level to ensure no sewage or agricultural runoff, no shipping, no heavy industry or forestry, and no urbanisation. The surrounding areas of sea also have to be vast enough to act as buffer zones protecting the water quality.

Combining their 13 acres of pristine Grade A shellfish protected waters with much valued advice from Peter Macaskill, the well-known mussel farmer on Skye, Andy and Jude aspire to make their mussel farm as eco friendly as possible, reducing their footprint on the environment to support marine diversity in the area. Already they have changed the plastic cup weights at the bottom of the droppers with biodegradable recycled paper ones, they are changing the petrol boat engines to electric, they have recycled the old ropes lying on the seabed, and the mussel farm is back up and running! With millions of spat on one rope alone, the Isle of Skye Mussel Company is in business.

There are the wider environmental benefits of mussel farming that Andy and Jude point out: each mussel filters approximately 25 litres of seawater a day, improving its quality and clarity; the droppers hanging from the mussel lines (roughly 600–800 droppers per line) gather seaweeds creating havens of protection for small fish; these droppers can also act as a means of wave energy dissipation, thereby providing protection from coastal erosion; and the tiny mussels that drop off the lines in storms provide food for the crabs and starfish, while the shell debris on the seabed provides additional habitats for smaller invertebrates.

Andy and Jude dive regularly to record the changes, test the water and measure the growth of their mussels. During these dives, they've seen lumpfish using the lines as shelters, pipefish blending with the seaweeds, shoals of mackerel and pollock darting through the dropper ropes and beautiful anemones, urchins, limpets and sea slugs.

In spite of their shared marine knowledge and conservation experience, Andy and Jude conclude that there is still much to be learnt about this amazing bivalve. What we do know for sure is that mussel cultivation has great benefits for the environment and for the health of those who add them to their plates too. Mussels are a rich source of protein, omega-3 fatty acid, vitamin B12 and the minerals iron, zinc and selenium.

Moules Marinière Two Ways

Classic French

If there is one mussel recipe I would never tire of, it is the classic Moules Marinière. Everything about it is perfect – from the simplicity of the method and ingredients to the joy of mopping up all the garlicky wine juices with fresh, crusty baguette. Some cooks add cream to the dish, which is delicious too, but I'm reserving that for the second way of preparing Moules Marinière – the Highland way! However, I think the classic French way is perfect for the harvest of the Isle of Skye Mussel Company.

Serves 4

———

roughly 1.75kg Isle of Skye fresh mussels

25g butter

2 shallots, finely chopped

2 garlic cloves, finely chopped

200ml crisp white wine

a small bunch of flat-leaf or curly parsley, finely chopped

sea salt and freshly ground black pepper

chunks of crusty baguette, to serve

Wash the mussels under plenty of cold, running water. Discard any open ones that won't close when lightly squeezed. Pull out any tough, fibrous beards and knock off the barnacles, if there are any.

Melt the butter in big pot – large enough and with a lid for all the mussels to steam – and add the shallots and garlic to soften.

Add the wine, bring to the boil and then toss in the mussels and half the parsley. Put the lid on, turn up the heat and steam the mussels for 3–4 minutes, shaking the pan from time to time, until all the mussels open.

Season with salt and pepper, sprinkle with the rest of the parsley, and serve immediately with the bread to mop up all the deliciousness.

Traditional Highland

Well, as you can imagine, the Highland Way involves whisky and why not? Choose a whisky you like, or from the locale you are in, and follow the recipe above, substituting the wine for whisky and adding 200ml double cream to temper it. Instead of parsley, add toasted oatmeal. Simply toast the oatmeal in the oven until it emits a toasted aroma and then add it at the end as you would the parsley in the traditional version. If you enjoy the taste of whisky, this is the one for you!

A handful of the Isle of Skye Mussel Company's pristine mussels.

Alasdair 'Bally' Philp

I truly believe we can have conservation and fisheries in the same place if we allow areas for low-impact fisheries that are not bottom trawling.

Surrounded by coastal communities all of his life and coming from a family of fishermen, Bally was born to be one. His earliest memory is of being on his dad's trawler as a wee lad catching demersal white fish, such as cod, whiting and monkish. When the numbers of white fish declined and prawns became the dominant catch, his father left commercial fishing to set up a factory processing them. For nearly 20 years, he was the principal buyer and seller of prawns in the north-west but, when the local fishing fleet declined due to lack of viability, there were no longer enough prawns to keep the business going so he had to close the factory.

Bally believes that the reason the numbers of white fish declined was due to large-scale bottom-trawling and dredging as both methods involve dragging gear along the seabed and disturbing it which has a huge impact on a wide range of species and the ecosystem, weakening the flora and fauna. 'It's like turning a healthy woodland into a ploughed field,' Bally says. 'This has made catching bottom-living white fish like cod and haddock more difficult and in many cases they have gone.' When Bally was younger he used to work with trawlers and scallop dredgers and recalls the long hours and harsh weather, how you had to become tough to cope with it. He never got over the killing of species that weren't commercially targeted but got caught and killed anyway. So, he prefers creel fishing as he finds it a selective and sustainable method with any by-catch going back into the water and surviving.

Now, almost all the inshore fishing of the north-west is based on shellfish, mainly prawns and scallops. Bally keeps his boat, *Nemesis* BRD 115, in Kyleakin and he and his two-man crew concentrate solely on prawns. He used to always export to Spain, France, Portugal and Italy but the distribution network for the fishing industry was severely affected by the pandemic lockdowns so locals got the chance to enjoy the seafood. Now Bally and the fishermen in his community are trying to find a balance, as they would rather sell to locals. When

the boats come into the pier with the fresh catch, the fishermen get a buzz from the gathering queue, ready to chat and buy the shellfish to take home, or to take to fish merchants in other parts of Scotland. Andy Richardson (p.206) is often there on his 'Scallop Express' run for David Lowrie Fish Merchants (p.203) in Fife.

In his lifetime as a fisherman on the west coast, Bally has seen the fishing change from netting herring to trawling white fish, to creel fishing for prawns (langoustines), and he feels strongly that the ecosystem of our seabed is in perpetual decline. As the National Coordinator of the Scottish Creel Fishermen's Federation (SCFF), he has one solution for this decline: to bring back the Victorian three-mile law to reserve spaces for low-impact fishing.

'I'm not suggesting that trawling should be banned and that fishing livelihoods should be swapped for conservation,' he points out, 'just that trawlers should be kept out of spaces where an alternative method is viable.' This, he feels, could contribute to the increase of fish stocks and a healthier fishing industry and perhaps still be a way of life for the next generation.

Alasdair Macleod on Langoustines (Stornoway)

Alasdair Macleod has spent the majority of his life in Lewis where he has had a varied and interesting career from head teacher of Aird Primary School on the east coast of the island to the Gaelic development officer for the local council in Stornoway and, in his retirement, chairman of the Outer Hebrides Inshore Fisheries Group. He has always enjoyed cooking. On a therapeutic level, Alasdair has found it de-stressing but it has also led to him writing food and drink columns for the *Stornoway Gazette* and contributing to a number of other local and Gaelic magazines and newspapers, as well as radio and TV. When MG Alba, the Gaelic arm of the BBC, first started, he co-presented a six-part cookery programme called *The Way to Food*, produced by Tern TV, and he has organised three food festivals at An Lanntair arts centre in Stornoway, so it has been no surprise that our conversations have often been about food. Herring are one of his favourite fish to cook and eat, and there are shoals of them in the sea lochs around the island, and when it comes to shellfish, for

Alasdair, 'the ultimate shellfish delicacy' is langoustine.

'It is difficult for us to believe today that, in relatively recent times, one of the most delicious and sought-after shellfish from our Scottish waters was discarded and thrown overboard by fishermen who regarded them as a useless "by-catch",' Alasdair explains. I remember Stornoway in the late 1960s and early 1970s when the harbour was crammed with all manner of well-maintained, spick-and-span boats when white fish and herring were the kings of the ocean. Prawns, as langoustines were disparagingly called, were largely regarded as a nuisance by the fishing fleet and dumped unceremoniously overboard and considered worthless. I had friends and relatives on the Stornoway fishing fleet, on the *Ripple*, the *Braes of Garry*, the *Fiery Cross* and the *Golden Sheaf*, and if they were in port on Mondays I was invited on board during school lunch hour. Soup, haddock and potatoes were always on the menu but never langoustines.

'How times have changed! Langoustines are now seen as the saviour of the depleted fishing fleet and the modern Macduff Shellfish factory situated on Goat Island, on the edge of Stornoway harbour, is keen to buy as many langoustines as the trawlers can catch. If you are lucky, sometimes a friendly fisherman will sling you up a plastic bag of langoustines, fresh from the hold, but the Islander Shellfish on the quay always has top-quality langoustines available when weather conditions allow the fleet to head for the Minch langoustine fishery grounds.'

Alasdair's Langoustine Bisque

Alasdair regards the sweet flavour and sumptuous texture of langoustines as far superior to its bigger and more expensive cousin, the lobster. When he gets the freshly landed langoustines out of the pristine waters of the Minch, he likes to grill them with garlicky lemon butter and then uses the heads and shells to make this bisque.

Serves 4–6

12 fresh langoustines

50g butter

1 onion, finely chopped

1 carrot, finely chopped

2 celery sticks, finely chopped

1 leek, white part, finely chopped

½ fennel bulb, finely chopped

Shell the langoustines and keep aside. Crush the shells for the bisque.

Melt the butter in a deep, heavy pan over a medium heat. Add the vegetables, herbs and garlic and cook for 10 minutes on a low heat till softened, stirring occasionally.

87

1 bay leaf

1 sprig tarragon

2 garlic cloves, crushed

75g tomato purée

4 tomatoes, roughly chopped

120ml cognac

100ml dry white wine

1.5 litres fish stock

120ml double cream

sea salt and freshly ground
black pepper

juice of ½ lemon

a pinch of cayenne pepper

snipped chives, to garnish

Add the crushed langoustine shells. Stir in the tomato purée, tomatoes, cognac, white wine and fish stock. Bring to the boil and simmer for 1 hour.

Leave to cool slightly and then ladle everything into a food processor. Blend in short bursts until the shells break into very small pieces.

Strain the liquid through a coarse sieve, pushing through as much as you can. Then pass it again through a fine mesh sieve.

Return the bisque to the heat and bring to the boil. Add the peeled, fresh langoustines to just cook through. Stir in the cream. Season to taste with salt and pepper and add the lemon juice and cayenne pepper.

Serve the bisque in warm bowls garnished with chopped chives.

Lewis Mackenzie

Perhaps best known as the sugar kelp diver and harvester for the Isle of Harris Distillery, Lewis Mackenzie is also the founder and owner of Hebridean Wildfoods which provides sustainably hand-harvested seaweeds from the cold, clean, Grade A Hebridean waters (p.80) to quality food processors, distributers and chefs nationwide. These seaweeds, which all have their own seasonal characteristics and require different harvesting techniques, include mermaid's lace; sea spaghetti, a delicious alternative to the pasta equivalent; pelvetia (also called 'sea sprigs'), which turns bright green when boiled and has a nutty flavour; red dulse, now in demand, smoked, as a vegan alternative to bacon; the punchy and spicy pepper dulse; winged kelp (also called dabberlocks or Atlantic wakame); and sugar kelp which makes a versatile *en papillote* wrap for baking fish, chicken or meat.

It is only the sugar kelp that is used as a key botanical in Harris Gin, and Lewis was asked by the Isle of Harris Distillery to source and harvest it in a sustainable way. So, after 35 years' experience as a scallop diver and boat charter provider, Lewis now finds himself anchoring over the sugar kelp sites and rolling into the cold water with mesh bags to collect the fronds. Back on board, he empties out the bags as each frond has to be cleaned and packed into boxes with ice packs before heading to Stornoway to be dried. He does this free-diving at low tide between January and May and harvests by

'pruning' the plant, enabling it to grow larger and stronger fronds which can reach three metres in length and one metre wide. During this harvesting time, he dives roughly three or four days a week, averaging 80 kilos of sugar kelp fronds a day. In spite of wearing a 5mm-thick drysuit, the water is undeniably cold, but Lewis tells me that the underwater adventures outweigh any discomfort. Even after three decades of exploring below the waves, he enjoys amazing sights and thrills like swimming alongside a sunfish and basking sharks.

Lewis's Sea Urchin Snack

Snack for 1

For the dressing

juice of 1 lime

2 tsp soy sauce

½ tsp wasabi paste

1 fresh sea urchin

4–5 wild gorse flowers

4–5 pepper dulse tips

When Lewis is out harvesting in the sea lochs and feeling a tad peckish, he makes himself a delicious on-the-go snack. He steps ashore to pick a handful of bright yellow, coconut-scented wild gorse flowers and takes some pepper dulse from the lower shore, then gets back on the boat to head to the rocky pools as it nears low tide to scoop up a couple of pretty, pink sea urchins. With a ready-made dressing on board, Lewis has everything he needs to prepare his snack.

Mix together the dressing ingredients in a small cup or jar.

Using a small, sharp knife, cut open the urchin around the base. Wash out the upper part of the shell containing the uni – the sea urchin roe – and remove any black film. Turn the shell upside down so the uni are facing you, drizzle with the dressing and garnish with the gorse flowers and pepper dulse. Enjoy!

Harris Gin and Beetroot Gravadlax

Curing fish in salt, sugar and spirit is such a lovely tradition in the islands and Highlands – in fact in the whole Nordic region. So, when on stunning Luskentyre beach, enjoying the miles of white sand and blue-green sea – sunshine and blue skies too, if you're lucky – slices of Hebridean salmon cured in Harris Gin on oatcakes with a Harris Gin and tonic in hand seems like a marriage made in heaven. Alternatively, a peaty whisky brings its own attributes and you could use a peaty sea salt. The addition of beetroot to the cure has become popular everywhere you go but it never ceases to make the slices of salmon look appetising.

Line a dish big enough for your salmon with a layer of aluminium foil and place both fillets, skin-side down in it. Rub the gin all over the fresh salmon. Mix together the sugar, salt and ground pepper, and scatter it over one of the salmon fillets and finish with the grated beetroot, then place the other fillet, skin-side up, on top, so that you create a salmon sandwich. Pull the foil over the fillets to create a parcel, place a weight on top – such as measuring weights, a small board or a flat stone from the garden – and place in the fridge for 2–4 days. During this time, you need to turn it occasionally and pour off any liquid seeping from the fish.

After 2–4 days, lift the salmon out of the foil, scrape off any of the cure and slice it finely, or thickly.

Serves 10–12, as a starter

1.2kg fresh, boned Hebridean salmon, in two big fillets but skin left on

200ml Harris Gin

150g granulated or soft brown sugar

100g Isle of Skye Sea Salt

1 tbsp black peppercorns, coarsely ground

2 beetroot, cleaned and grated

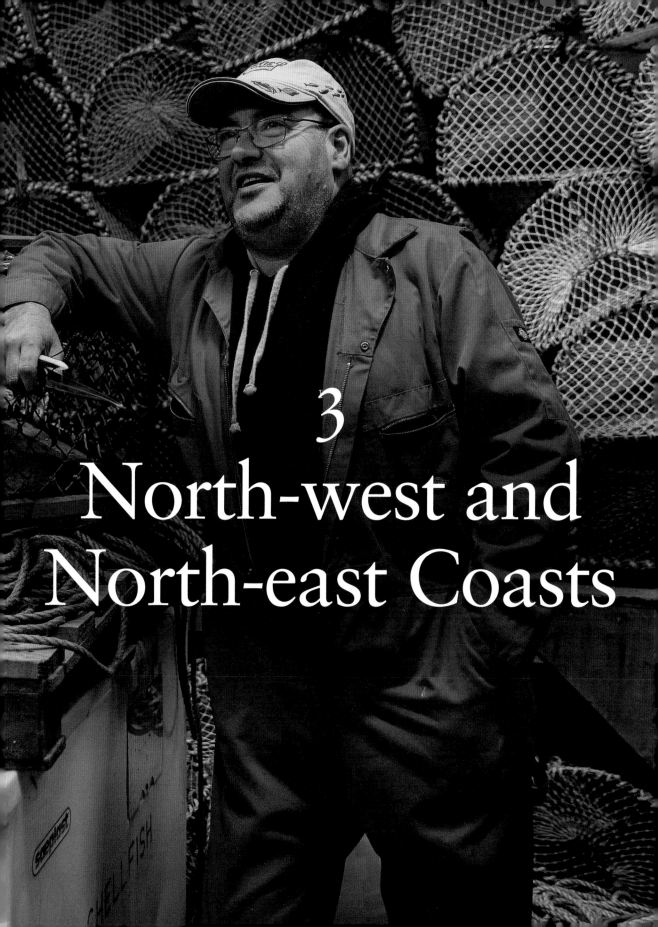

3
North-west and North-east Coasts

The north coast is navigated by a single road – the North Coast 500 – along which there are many old herring ports and active fishing harbours. In the west, the coastline is rugged and deeply incised with penetrating sea lochs as you pass through Ullapool, Lochinver and Kinlochbervie, where fish is sold through the port's auction market. From Durness to Wick, which was one of the busiest ports at the height of the herring trade, you pass by Scrabster with its long history of sail, steam and large trawlers berthing for shelter or repairs on passage to St Kilda, Shetland and Iceland. Scrabster is still a top landing port with a fish market and the main ferry terminal to Orkney. Travelling down the north-east coast, there are still remnants of the now-banned salmon netting stations, as well as ice houses and bothies around the Easter Ross peninsula, and by the Dornoch and Moray Firths where the land shelves gently to the sea. The north-east coast could not be more different to the north-west.

Singapore Spineys

This dish is based on the traditional chilli crab that is a great favourite in the food stalls and coffee houses of Singapore. There, it is served as a communal dish and is finger-licking messy, so you do need a bowl of warm water for cleaning your fingers. In place of crab, I am using spineys (squat lobsters) as they are quick to cook and less messy to eat than crab and I thought it was a good way to enjoy the spineys that we picked up on Dry Island when filming Appetite for Adventure *(see p.96) in the north-west.*

To get the background kick and richness of the chillies, you need to soak them ahead of time for at least 6–8 hours.

Drain the chillies and squeeze them to get rid of any excess water and most of the seeds. Using a mortar and pestle pound the chillies with the garlic and ginger to a coarse paste with the salt. Add the shallots and keep pounding. Beat in the dry-roasted shrimp paste.

Heat the oil in a wok, or wide, heavy-based pot, and stir in the spice paste. Keep stirring until fragrant and slightly caramelised. Stir in the tomato purée for a minute, then add the ketchup, soy sauce, vinegar and jaggery. Pour in the stock and bring the liquid to the boil, stirring all the time. Reduce the heat and simmer for 10 minutes. Toss in the coriander and season to taste. Meanwhile, bring a separate pot of water to the boil. Drop in the spiney tails for no more than a minute. Drain and plunge them into a bowl cold water to stop the cooking.

Crack the eggs into the reduced sauce and lightly scramble. Toss in the spiney tails, coating them in the sauce. Scatter the spring onions and reserved coriander over the top.

Enjoy eating with your fingers by pulling the flesh out from the tail and dipping it back in the sauce. Mop up the extra sauce with chunks of crusty bread.

Serves 2

For the spice paste

4 dried red and 2 dried smoky chillies (for example, chipotle or ancho), soaked in boiling water for a minimum of 6–8 hours, or overnight

4 garlic cloves, roughly chopped

a large thumb-sized piece of fresh ginger, peeled and roughly chopped

1 tsp Isle of Skye Sea Salt

2 shallots, finely chopped

1 tsp shrimp paste, dry roasted in a pan

---

2 tbsp vegetable, rapeseed or light sesame oil

2 tbsp tomato purée

2 tbsp tomato ketchup

2 tbsp naturally brewed soy sauce

2 tbsp white wine vinegar

1 tbsp jaggery or muscovado sugar

300ml shellfish or chicken stock

a bunch of fresh coriander, finely chopped (reserve some for garnishing)

sea salt and freshly ground black pepper

12–16 spineys, remove the head from the tails before cooking

2 eggs, beaten

2 spring onions, trimmed and finely sliced

Dry Island Langoustines Pan-fried
with Garlic, Juniper, Wild Herbs and Wine

Serves 3–4

———

roughly 24 langoustines, kept at –1°C to stun them into hibernation before cooking

150g butter

6 plump garlic cloves, finely chopped

a few juniper berries, crushed

several sprigs of wild thyme

several sprigs of bog myrtle

a fistful of sweet cicely, roughly chopped

a fistful of spignel, roughly chopped

a glass of white wine

sea salt and freshly ground black pepper

In June 2022, when I was travelling up the west Highland coast, I was involved in making the cycling film Appetite for Adventure, *produced by Hostelling Scotland and the Adventure Syndicate showcasing an alternative route to the North Coast 500 whilst sourcing local produce to cook in the hostels. For shellfish we headed to Dry Island where Ian McWhinney runs Shellfish Safaris in his creel boat. He had been out that day and had returned with several crabs, some spineys (squat lobster) and a bucketful of langoustines. We headed to the hostel in Gairloch (where the kitchen is better kitted out than my own!) and cooked them up with wild herbs that we had gathered on the way. If you can't pick wild herbs, use a mix of garden herbs instead, such as chives, marjoram, hyssop, parsley and mint.*

———

Bring a pot of seawater, or generously salted tap water, to a rolling boil and drop in the langoustines, making sure they are completely submerged, and cook for about 4 minutes – depending on the size of your pot you may have to cook them in batches. The shells will deepen in colour and the flesh should turn white and opaque. Drain and plunge into a bowl of cold water if not using immediately.

Prepare two large frying pans – you will be using both at the same time. Divide the butter between them, melt it and stir in the garlic, split between the two pans, for 1 minute. Add the sprigs of herbs and most of the chopped ones.

Drain the langoustines and immediately transfer them to the pan, tossing them in the butter and herbs for 2 minutes. Add the wine, season with sea salt and black pepper, and toss in the rest of the chopped herbs.

Bring the pans to the table and eat with your fingers, shelling and dipping the cooked flesh back into the garlicky, herby and buttery wine juices at the bottom of the pan – you'll need some crusty bread to help mop it all up. Keep your shells for a bisque or a stock.

Ruby's Creole Fish Patties
(Gairloch)

Makes 6 small patties

225g white fish fillets (cod, haddock, coley)

2 spring onions, chopped

1 tsp curry powder

½ tsp paprika

a pinch of cayenne pepper

a handful of fresh coriander, finely chopped

zest and juice of 1 lime

sea salt and freshly ground black pepper

2 large eggs

vegetable oil, for shallow frying

The Black Pearl Creole Kitchen is one of my favourite eating spots on the North Coast 500. It has grown from its moveable horse box, which still pops up at different locations in Wester Ross with queues lured by the aroma of warming spices in Anji Locke's dishes and happy to stand in the rain, to the permanent shelter of an old café in Gairloch which has been refurbished and decorated by Anji's husband, sons and friends. The customer feedback has been amazing as locals and international visitors tuck into the fusion of local produce combined with the flavours of Barbados and Dominica where Anji's parents are from. In fact, these lightly spiced fish patties were created by Anji's mum, Ruby, who would buy fish at the local fish market near The Briggait in Glasgow's Tollcross, and then pep it up with the flavours she was missing from home when she first came to live in this country. They are delicious both hot and cold, so we took them to eat while cycling up the coast. In the Black Pearl Creole Kitchen they are served with a choice of herb yoghurt or hot pepper sauce.

Place the fish in a steamer for about 8 minutes so that it cooks gently but remains moist. Leave it to cool and then flake the fish into a bowl.

Add the rest of the ingredients, apart from the eggs, to the bowl and season generously with the salt and pepper.

In a separate bowl, whisk the eggs and gradually add them to the fish so that the mixture has the consistency of cake batter. (If your mixture is too dry, whisk another egg and add as much of it as you need.)

Heat enough oil in a non-stick frying pan to shallow fry. Keep the pan on a medium temperature and place a heaped tablespoon of the fish batter into pan. The mixture should hold its shape with a little spread. Fry two or three patties at time for 2 minutes each side, so that they turn golden brown and crispy around the edges.

Serve them hot, or at room temperature, with wedges of lemon to squeeze over them and a hot or herb yoghurt sauce of your choice.

Haggis-stuffed Mackerel
Baked in Newspaper

Wrapping fish in newspaper to cook it in the fire is an old fishing trick. By dampening the paper in water, the fish cooks slowly inside until the paper dries out and when unwrapped the skin peels away. All you need is a campfire, some newspaper, one or two line-caught mackerel or trout, and a good haggis – as I was travelling through the north-west I picked up my favourite one, made by Ritchies' Aultbea in Mellon Charles.

Put the whole haggis into a pot of water and place it over the fire to boil gently for about 30 minutes.

While the haggis is cooking, prepare the fish. Using a sharp knife, remove the guts and then slit the underside of the fish from below the head to the tail. Carefully press the area around the backbone to prise it away from the flesh, then snap it with your fingers at each end and pull it out, keeping the fish intact. Rinse the fish inside and out and pat dry.

Slit the haggis casing open and leave to cool a little before stuffing it into the fish, filling the cavity completely. You can hold the two sides of the fish together by threading a thin stick through them or, if you've caught two fish, you can place them in the newspaper with their full bellies touching each other. Wet the newspaper before wrapping up the fish and place it in the hot embers to cook.

The cooking time will vary according to the size of your fish and how hot the embers are so the best way to gauge it is by the newspaper – once it has dried out, unwrap the fish and enjoy the cooked flesh with the hot haggis.

Josh Talbot

Located on the east shore of Loch Broom, Ullapool was founded as a herring port in 1788 for the fleets fishing the Minch and the Atlantic, and some of the old curing sheds still exist. Today it is a picturesque gateway to the Outer Hebrides with a regular ferry service to Stornoway, a popular mooring for yachts and a busy fishing port with ten white-fish boats landing regularly, two crabbing boats coming in each week, five prawn trawlers and seven inshore creel boats. Josh Talbot is co-owner of one of these creel boats, the *Bon Ami* UL77, which was transported by lorry all the way from Jersey in 2018.

Josh spent his early years in Cape Wrath, where his father surveyed nesting birds for the RSPB, and went to Achfary Primary School before attending high school in Ullapool. He didn't do any fishing when he was young but he enjoyed mucking about in the water, doing a bit of sailing and surfing. When he was 23 years old he joined the five-man crew on *Heather K* owned by Heddle Costie (p.106), also co-owner of the 10-metre creel boat *Bon Ami*, and realised he loved fishing. The rota for the crew on the *Heather K* was four weeks on and two weeks off. They would travel to the west side of Lewis and out to St Kilda and the Flannan Isles to fish for crabs and lobsters, dropping 1,200 creels a day. Josh will never forget the day they dropped 400 lobster creels on their way around the Flannan Isles and found 398 big lobsters in them when they lifted them that afternoon. The Flannan Isles may be best known for the mysterious disappearance of the three lighthouse keepers in 1900 but, for Josh, they will always be associated with lobsters.

Now, creel fishing full time on *Bon Ami*, Josh's day begins early, checking the creels and pots for the crabs, lobsters and langoustines that have been drawn by the bait. For the crabs and lobsters, Josh catches fish or uses the fishmonger's scraps for bait, but for the langoustines he salts herring to draw out the strong-smelling oils, which they love. Josh has to check his creels and pots every two or three days to get the catch out and put fresh bait in but also to make sure they haven't been eaten by octopus or starfish, which are the main predators and will happily work their way through the pots and creels, killing and devouring all the shellfish. He only takes the

good-sized crabs, lobsters and langoustines that he has caught, returning small ones to the seabed, and if any other fish have got into his
creels or pots he releases them so that they survive.

Most of Josh's catch goes off in the van with Mark Renwick, who
operates the langoustine run from west to east for Keltic Seafare
(p.121), but he also supplies the busy Seafood Shack (p.109), run by
his partner, Kirsty, and Mark's wife, Fenella. It is a tight-knit fishing
community in Ullapool where for many the fishing is not just a job,
it's an enjoyable way of life. Like many others, Josh would like to
see better management of the fishing industry on the west coast. He
has great hopes for his baby daughter to follow in his footsteps.

Octopus and Bean Stew with Bog Myrtle and Salsa Verde

In some Mediterranean countries, octopus is just as popular as squid or langoustines – chargrilled and served with a citrusy dressing, fried or in fish stew. I think I have eaten more octopus in Sicily than anywhere else so this recipe is based on a fisherman's stew I've had there. The freshly harpooned octopus was simmered slowly to tenderise it and then seared at the end. As octopus seems to be one of the main predators of shellfish caught in creels around our coast, perhaps we should eat it more, as is the custom along the Mediterranean coast. If you don't have any bog myrtle near you, just use bay leaves.

Serves 3–4

For the salsa verde

a handful of flat-leaf parsley, stalks included

a handful of fresh mint leaves

6–8 chives

2 tsp capers, drained of vinegar or brine

2 preserved anchovy fillets, drained of oil

1 tbsp red wine vinegar

juice of ½ lemon

120ml olive oil

sea salt and freshly ground black pepper

---

1 octopus, roughly 1.5kg

1 onion, coarsely chopped

a handful of bog myrtle, or bay leaves

3–4 garlic cloves, crushed

2 tsp coriander seeds

200ml white wine

1½ tins (roughly 700g) plum tomatoes

1 tsp pul biber, Aleppo pepper, or dried chilli flakes

1 tsp sugar or honey

2 × 400g tins cannellini beans, rinsed and drained

1 tbsp chopped green olives

1 tbsp capers, drained of vinegar

olive oil

sea salt and freshly ground black pepper

Parmesan, for grating

You can prepare the salsa verde ahead of time or while the octopus is cooking. Put the herbs into a blender with the capers, anchovies, vinegar and lemon juice and start to whizz, then gradually add the olive oil in steady stream with the machine running so that the sauce thickens. Season to taste with salt and pepper and put aside.

Put the octopus, onion, bog myrtle, garlic and coriander seeds into a pot. Add just enough water to cover the octopus and bring to the boil. Reduce the heat, cover and simmer for about 1½ hours, until the octopus is tender. Turn off the heat and leave the octopus to cool in the liquid.

When cool, lift the octopus out of the pot and onto a board. Add the wine to the liquid in the pot, bring it to the boil then simmer for 10 minutes to reduce it. Add the tomatoes with the pul biber, or dried chillies, and sugar and continue to simmer until the mixture is thick and saucy – you will need to break the tomatoes up a bit with your spoon. Add the cannellini beans, olives and capers, and season with salt and pepper.

Meanwhile, slice the head off the octopus and keep it for a stock. Keep the legs whole and rub them with olive oil and salt. Heat a heavy-based pan and sear the legs for 2 minutes each side. Slice them into two or three pieces and toss them through the bean and tomato mixture.

Serve the stew in bowls with spoonfuls of salsa verde, a dusting of Parmesan and chunks of crusty bread to mop up the sauce.

Coconut, Turmeric and Lime Broth with Shellfish and Hake

Coconut-milk broths spiked with chillies, ginger and lemongrass are a feature Southern Indian and South-east Asian cooking, and work so well with the fresh fish and shellfish from Scottish waters. The key to a good broth of this nature is the base paste, known as the rempah in Singapore and Malaysia, as this is where all the flavour comes from. Once you have the broth seasoned to your taste, all you have to do is drop in the seafood of your choice. In this recipe I'm using langoustines, mussels and hake but you can use whatever your fishmonger or fish van has on the day.

First make the rempah. Using a mortar and pestle, pound the chillies, ginger, garlic and lemongrass with the salt to coarse paste. Add the lime zest, coriander leaves and shrimp paste and pound until almost smooth.

Heat the coconut oil in a large wok, or a large, heavy-based pot. Stir in the shallots for 2 minutes to soften, then stir in the spice paste. Keep stirring, until the paste emits a lovely aroma, then stir in the jaggery and the turmeric. Add the lime juice so that the spices don't burn on the base of the wok or pot, then pour in the coconut milk. Bring the liquid to the boil, stirring gently from time to time, then reduce the heat and simmer with the lid on for 25–30 minutes to allow the flavours to mingle.

Stir in the fish sauce with half the fresh coriander and the lime leaves and then drop in the shellfish and chunks of fish and cook gently for 2–3 minutes. Remember both the fish and shellfish will continue to cook in the hot broth in your bowl.

Ladle the broth into bowls, scatter the rest of the chopped coriander over the top, and serve with a segment of lime to squeeze into the broth.

Serves 4–6

For the rempah

1–2 fresh red chillies, deseeded and roughly chopped

2 large thumb-sized pieces of fresh ginger, peeled and roughly chopped

4 plump garlic cloves, roughly chopped

4 lemongrass stalks, trimmed of their outer leaves and tough base, and very finely sliced so that you don't get long, stringy fibres in the paste

1 tsp Isle of Skye Sea Salt

zest of 2 limes

a small bunch of coriander leaves, roughly chopped

1 tsp shrimp paste

1 tbsp coconut oil

2–3 shallots, peeled and finely chopped

2 tsp jaggery or light muscovado sugar

1 tbsp ground turmeric

juice of 2 limes

4 × 400ml tins coconut milk

1 tbsp fish sauce

a bunch of fresh coriander, finely chopped

a few fresh lime leaves, optional

225g fresh langoustines, shelled if you wish

225g fresh mussels

225g fresh hake, halibut, coley or monkfish, cut into bite-size chunks

sea salt

2–4 limes, cut into segments

Heddle Costie

Heddle is a busy fisherman with one foot in Ullapool, the other in Orkney. He lives in Ullapool where he met his lovely wife, Julie, when he came into harbour to land his catch one day, but he grew up on Westray. His father was a fisherman and creel maker on Westray and he built the lobster ponds there, but with a surname name like 'Costie' there is likely to be Spanish ancestry in the family, dating back to the Spanish Armada in 1588, when survivors of wrecked ships settled on Westray and ended up marrying local Orcadian women. Heddle himself could pass for a Spaniard.

When Heddle left school, he went to Inverness to do a course on fish farming but by the early 1990s the price of salmon took a dive so he returned to Westray to work on the creel boats until he could afford his own. His first was *Heather K*, a crab boat with a five-man crew which took week-long trips to rocky islands, like the Flannan Isles, roughly 17 nautical miles west of the Isle of Lewis, to get lobsters and crabs. They had to go that distance as the land up the north-west coast and the eastern side of Lewis falls into mud in the Minch, ideal for prawns but not for the other crustaceans. Josh Talbot (p.101) was one of the crew working for Heddle at the height of his pre-pandemic crab-fishing days, when they were busy supplying 1,000 boxes a week to China, an export business that required so much time-consuming paperwork that Julie had a full-time job sorting out the complex labelling and environmental certificates for shipping livestock and attaining the correct stamps from the Chamber of Commerce.

Heddle now has two boats: the *Lady K*, which he keeps in Ullapool from November to May for the lobster creels, but takes up to Orkney for the summer to catch lobsters there; and *Bon Ami*, which he co-owns with Josh and which stays in Ullapool all year round, mainly for langoustines, but also for lobsters and crabs. Josh is in charge of a three-man crew when Heddle is in Orkney, where he is co-owner of QA (Quality Assured) Shellfish in Kirkwall, special-ising in the sale of live scallops and lobsters, most of which go down to Billingsgate Market in London. His business partner there is Robert Williamson who also owns QA Fish, a processor of fish caught and landed in Shetland. As Heddle has one foot in Ullapool, he has ensured he can leave QA Shellfish in the trusted hands of

manager Stewart Grey. On the day I visited QA Shellfish in Kirkwall, Stewart was busy showing a group around the lobster and scallop ponds and packaging as they were interested in transporting large boxes of live lobsters and scallops to London by drone. I had encountered the same group earlier that day at the Orkney Fisherman's Society in Stromness so I now had visions of live shellfish flying through our skies in polystyrene boxes which, to be perfectly honest, is not far from the proposed reality.

Heddle also makes traditional creels, a skill he learned from his father in Westray. In the past, when fishing was stormed off, a creel fisherman would make and maintain his own gear. Heddle explained to me that the creels for lobsters and crabs need to be heavy, made with steel frames and polypropylene string, as they are laid in rock and kelp beds and get buffed about by the tides, whereas langoustine creels are lighter so that they sit on the mud in a sea loch and don't sink into it. Herring is the main bait used for all of the crustaceans so Heddle buys 24 pallets of it at time, freezes it in kilo blocks and puts it into the creels frozen or salted along with fish scraps from the fishmongers. On the days Heddle isn't fishing he goes to his Ullapool sheds to make these creels, which get used on his boats, and by QA Shellfish up in Orkney too.

Seafood Shack Lobster Arancini with Sweet Cherry Tomato and Basil Dip

You can't pass through Ullapool without stopping at the Seafood Shack. Since opening in 2016, it has become a food tourism institution! The two owners, Kirsty Scobie and Fenella Renwick, set up the Shack as a way to hold on to and enjoy some of the amazing catch being landed by the fishing boats in Ullapool but which was immediately being loaded onto trucks to head south. Supply wasn't a problem as Fenella's husband, Mark, who takes the landed west-coast langoustines to Keltic Seafare (p.121) on the east coast, is also a part-time fisherman, and Kirsty's partner, Josh (p.101), is out in his fishing boat Bon Ami *almost every day and drops off whatever he has caught. This means the menu at the Shack is often decided in the morning, depending on how many lobsters, crabs and langoustines are dropped off by Josh and how many scallops are provided by local diver Gary Lewis. Most of the white fish is sourced locally too. When it comes to the packaging, local, sustainable and compostable are at the heart of the Seafood Shack's ethos and their freshly prepared seafood has won awards, has been showcased in their best-selling book and has featured in a TV programme with Mary Berry!*

Serves 6

For the arancini

2 medium-sized live lobsters, or you could use already cooked ones

150g sea salt

100g butter

1 white onion, finely chopped

3 garlic cloves, crushed

1 vegetable stock cube

450g risotto rice

225ml white wine

4 sprigs of thyme

600ml boiling water

140g cup of frozen peas

80g Parmesan, grated

2 tbsp parsley, finely chopped

sea salt and freshly ground black pepper

300g flour

6 medium eggs, whisked

roughly 12 slices of white bread, ground into crumbs

1200 ml vegetable oil

Put a large pot of water on to boil for the lobsters and add your salt.

Drop in your lobsters and cook for 8 minutes, drain and leave to cool.

Place the lobsters on a board, break off the claws and knuckles and pull off the tail. (The head, small legs and anything left over can be made into a delicious bisque.) Cut the tail lengthways down the middle and remove the meat. Make an incision in the middle of both sides of the claws and then hit them (use a cleaver if you have one or the back of a heavy knife) to crack them open and remove the meat, being aware of the cartilage in the middle. Break the knuckles in half (again using a cleaver or back of the knife) and pick out the meat. Chop all the meat into small chunks and keep aside.

Put a large frying pan on a high heat, add half your butter, white onion and garlic. Lower the heat and sweat, mixing constantly so

For the cherry tomato dip

1 red onion, roughly chopped

2 garlic cloves crushed

600g cherry tomatoes

3 tsp sugar

1 tbsp white wine vinegar

6 basil leaves

sea salt and freshly ground black pepper

rocket leaves, shaved Parmesan and lemon wedges, for garnishing

they don't burn, until the onions are soft. Toss in the vegetable stock cube and rice for a few minutes, then add the wine and thyme. Once the rice has absorbed the wine, add 200ml of the boiling water. Keep adding 200ml at a time until all the water has been absorbed and the rice has a bite to it. Now, toss in the peas, Parmesan and half of the parsley and leave to cool completely.

While your risotto is cooling, make your dip. Heat the rest of the butter in a pan and sweat off the red onions and garlic. Once the onions have softened, add the cherry tomatoes and cook until soft and falling apart. Add the sugar, vinegar and basil, season well, and whizz in a food blender to a smooth paste.

Once your rice is completely cool, mix in your chunks of lobster, check the seasoning, and start making the arancini by moulding the mixture into balls that weigh roughly 80g each.

Put the flour, eggs and breadcrumbs in three separate bowls. Season them all and toss the rest of the parsley through the bread-crumbs. Coat the arancini in the flour, then the eggs, then the bread-crumbs, making sure to keep your hands clean throughout to stop the mixture sticking (it helps to wear blue catering gloves). Place your arancini balls on baking paper on a tray.

Pour the vegetable oil into a medium-sized pan – one that is wide and deep enough to deep-fry the arancini in batches – and place over a low-medium heat. Try to heat the oil to 170°C; if you don't have a thermometer, simply test the temperature by dropping in a small corner of bread – if it sizzles then it is hot enough. Fry your arancini in batches by lowering them into the oil and cooking for approxi-mately 8 minutes, until dark gold in colour – if they go dark too quickly, turn the temperature of your oil down.

Drain the arancini on kitchen paper and serve with your cherry tomato dip, rocket leaves, shaved Parmesan and lemon wedges.

Netta

Netta UL85 is a much-loved creel boat moored in Ardmair, just north of Ullapool. Sandy Watters bought her from Cheetah Marine in 1995, ten years after he had started fishing, and named her after his mother. At that time, Cheetah Marine was a new company and only sold boats of 6.2 metres in length but Sandy persuaded them to lengthen *Netta* to 6.9 metres and, as far as he knows, she was the first catamaran of that size to fish commercially around Ullapool and the west coast. Now it's probably the company's best-selling size of vessel. The onboard fishing arrangements are designed for single-handed operation and that is how Sandy used her for the next 26 years.

Although Sandy grew up in Oban by the sea, he didn't start fishing until he moved to Ullapool with his young family to join his wife who had taken up the post of art teacher in the local secondary school. He began as a crewman on a small, two-handed creel boat when the Klondykers, the big rusty factory ships from the communist states, were still coming into Ullapool's harbour to process mackerel to take back to East Germany and the USSR before the end of the Cold War. During this time, there could be as many as 70 Klondykers moored in Loch Broom, and Ullapool was busy and buzzing with fishermen and seafood and plenty of cheap bait for the creel boats.

The Klondykers had left by the time Sandy bought *Netta*, and during his years with her he would fish for lobsters, velvet crabs and whelks, but over 90 per cent of his effort was targeting prawns (langoustines). Sandy's prawns even featured in Ching He Huang's BBC cooking show, *Chinese Food Made Easy*, when the Taiwanese-born chef cooked them for Sandy on board *Netta*. When a local lad had the opportunity to buy a second-hand fishing vessel through the Young Fisherman's Entrant Scheme set up by the Marine Fund Scotland, Sandy saw this as an opportunity to retire and meet the needs of the young entrant, enabling him to buy the boat and business as a going concern.

That lad was Louis Neate. As a schoolboy, Louis had gone out in the sea near Ullapool in his kayak with his own creels to catch lobsters and crabs, and dreamed of having his own boat one day. But when he left school that dream seemed unattainable, and he went off to work on a sheep station in the Falklands, travelled and fished

in New Zealand, and worked for Joe Hayes at Ockran Oysters back in Ullapool for three years. From time to time, Louis also worked with Sandy on *Netta*. So, with a generosity of heart that Louis is deeply grateful for, Sandy helped him secure a grant from the Marine Fund Scotland, which contributed 75 per cent of the £28,000 purchase price. Louis had to find that amount again to cover the licence, which enables him to fish for lobsters, crabs, langoustines and hand-line mackerel.

Louis became the proud owner and skipper of *Netta* in 2022. Out in his yellow and blue boat with 680 creels and fishing grounds around Ardmair and Isle Martin, he fishes for a living but, like Sandy, he also sees it as a way of life. When he's not fishing, Louis is busy with repairs and maintenance and plans to fit a self-shooting table so that, instead of manually throwing the creels off the boat into the water, they go down a ramp by themselves. Using herring and fish scraps as bait, he averages a land of 40 kilos a day, two to three days a week, as the creels need to remain on the seabed for a couple of days before lifting. Louis can't leave them for too long as the octopus and starfish will devour the shellfish while trapped in the creels.

Like all the prawn (langoustine) fisherman in the Ullapool area, who tend to work together rather than in competition, Louis sells his catch to Mark Renwick who operates the langoustine run from west to east for Keltic Seafare (p.121). As for Sandy, he may miss the fishing but he has the joy of seeing *Netta* moored in front of his house every day and the satisfaction of knowing she is well cared for.

Klondyker Shellfish Stew

The colourful history of the Klondykers anchored in Ullapool, with the ships' lights brightening up Loch Boom at night and large crews from vodka-drinking nations on board, made me think this would be a good name for a fiery stew, packed with shellfish from the local creel boats and all the ingredients of a Bloody Mary!

Serves 4–6

2 tbsp olive oil

2 onions, finely chopped

3–4 garlic cloves, finely chopped

2 tsp pul biber, Aleppo chilli or dried chilli flakes

2 × 400g tins plum tomatoes

2 tsp sugar

1 red bell pepper, deseeded and chopped

600ml fish or chicken stock

300ml vodka

sea salt and freshly ground black pepper

a bunch of fresh coriander, finely chopped

roughly 500g freshly shucked oysters or mussels

roughly 500g shelled prawns

roughly 500g squid, cut into rings

Lea & Perrins Worcestershire sauce, Tabasco sauce to serve

Heat 1 tablespoon of oil in a heavy-based pot or wok and fry half the onions and all the garlic until soft. Add the pul biber and 1 tin of tomatoes with 1 teaspoon of sugar and cook to a thick pulp. Tip the pulp into a blender and whizz until smooth.

Heat the remaining tablespoon of oil in a heavy-based pot or wok and stir in the rest of the onions with the chopped pepper for 2–3 minutes. Add the second tin of plum tomatoes with the rest of the sugar and pour in the stock and vodka. Bring the liquid to the boil, then turn down the heat and simmer for about 30 minutes.

Stir in the whizzed sauce, bring the liquid back to the boil and season to taste. Add in half the coriander and then add in whatever shellfish you're using for roughly 2–3 minutes to make sure they are cooked through.

Ladle the thick stew into bowls, garnish with the rest of the coriander and serve with chunks of crusty bread to dunk into it. Pass around the Worcestershire sauce and Tabasco to splash into the stew.

Johnson and Loftus (Ullapool)

When I visited Dan Johnson and Tim Loftus in their busy boatyard, all activity seemed to be centred around a beautifully restored herring drifter, *St Vincent*, thought to be the only lug-rigged sailing Zulu still in existence. The Zulus, named after the Zulu War in Africa, originated in Lossiemouth on the Moray coast in 1879 and were magnificent, highly evolved herring luggers taking in the best features of two other Scottish fishing boats, the Scaffies and the Fifies. Sporting colossal, aerodynamically efficient lug sails – two masts and three sails – the Zulus were fast and powerful in the stormy seas of the north and east at a time when fortunes could be made or lost by the speed of landing the catch. At the height of the herring season this type of boat would have dropped the sails at night and drifted with the nets. At first light the crew would have hauled the nets on board with as much as 20 tons of herring, hoisted the sails and raced back to shore where the fisher wives would gut, salt and pack the herring.

The *St Vincent* was built in 1910 in Banff for a family out in Barra, where she worked as a herring boat in her early years. It is thought that she was later used for smuggling whisky from the ss *Politician* when it sank off the Hebridean island of Eriskay in 1941 – the incident which inspired Compton Mackenzie to write *Whisky Galore*. She has now been lovingly restored for a private collector with great attention to detail – even the bow and stern spars for setting the sails which lend the 50-foot wooden vessel an extra 40 feet in length – but she will also go back into the water as Dan and Tim and a three-man crew have plans to sail her from Ullapool to Tanera Mor, the largest of the Summer Isles. It should be an exciting voyage, a short one compared to the adventurous sailing experiences that both Dan and Tim have under their belts. Between them, they have sailed to Iceland, Greenland, down the coast of Africa and over to South America and the Caribbean, single-handedly and with their wives. The voyage on *St Vincent*, however, will be deeply satisfying as they will have brought a piece of history, an important part of our fishing heritage, back to life. Tim is also obsessed with herring so he will no doubt throw out a net on the journey.

The boat-building site of Johnson and Loftus, located just south of Ullapool with a slipway and hard standing for about 25 boats, a

hydraulic trailer and marine railway is a bit like a big boys' toy shed as Dan and Tim are simply doing what they loved doing as kids, only on a much bigger scale. Tim built his first traditional boat – a willow-framed coracle – when he was six years old. The first boat he bought had been built by a family who emigrated in it from South Africa and that inspired him to build his own and go to boat-building college. Dan grew up in his father's workshop, learning about timber and tools, ended up studying design and furniture construction in Edinburgh, and met Tim when he got in touch to ask his advice about buying an old boat.

Together, they can tackle the repairs and building of almost anything and their ambition is to recreate *Muirneag* SY486, the last big Scottish Zulu to fish solely under sail. Meaning 'darling girl' in Gaelic, *Muirneag* was built in Portessie, near Buckie, in 1903 and had a formidable reputation as a fast and able sailor under her hard-driving captain, Alexander 'Sandy' Macleod from Stornoway, who skippered her for 42 years. At the end of her life, she was broken up and her wood used as fence posts on the Isle of Lewis. Dan and Tim hope that her recreation will be at the heart of an educational and cultural heritage project on the role herring fishing played in world history.

Sweet-cured Herring with Juniper Berries and Spignel

Serves 4

8 herring fillets

50g Isle of Skye Sea Salt

2 red onions, very finely sliced

a handful of spignel, or dill, sprigs

200ml red or white wine vinegar

200g granulated or soft brown sugar

a handful of black peppercorns

a handful of ripe juniper berries

Since Ullapool's history is entwined with herring fishing boats and the 'herring lassies' skilfully gutting and salting them, and now two professional boat builders are restoring and recreating beautiful wooden fishing vessels, I can't leave the town without writing a herring recipe. Here is an easy way to salt and cure herring at home – a sweet cure with wild juniper berries and spignel (dill or fennel fronds will do instead). If you're not accustomed to filleting fish, just ask your fishmonger to prepare the herring for you.

Place the herring fillets, skin-side down, in a dish and sprinkle with the salt. Scatter the onions and spignel sprigs over them. Heat the vinegar and sugar in a saucepan with the peppercorns and juniper berries. Stir to make sure the sugar has dissolved and simmer for 5 minutes. Leave to cool.

Pour the cooled pickling liquid over the herring, cover, and chill for at least 24 hours. If you can, leave them for 3–4 days.

Lift the herring fillets out of the marinade and serve whole, or in thick, diagonally sliced pieces, with dill or lemon mayonnaise and chunks of crusty bread or oatcakes.

Cape Wrath Oysters

We farm oysters in Scotland's far north-west.

Never a truer word! As we approached the end of our cycling journey in the north-west, filming *Appetite for Adventure* (see p.96) for Hostelling Scotland and the Adventure Syndicate, we headed up the Kyle of Durness with oysters and whisky on our minds – a combination that makes the most perfect pairing for coastal distilleries with that hint of sea breeze and salt in their expressions. We had a bottle of smoky Bad na h-Achlaise that we had picked up from Badachro Distillery near Gairloch earlier on the trip, so we collected oysters from Cape Wrath Oysters and enjoyed them cooked on a fire on a beach in Durness with swigs of whisky (see photo p.xiii). Shucked and placed back into the deeper half shell, their own little cooking pot, with a drizzle of melted butter combined with wild herbs poured over them, they were utterly delicious and the perfect way to end the film and our trip. A whisky and oyster pairing made in heaven!

Passionate about oysters and their great sustainability credentials, Patrick and Lucy Blow founded Cape Wrath Oysters in 2014. Together they have around 50 years of broad experience in seafood, from fish farming in Africa and around the globe to wild-capture expertise, including the sourcing, quality, processing and retail of farmed and wild seafood. Oysters take between three and five years to grow to market size in the UK so Cape Wrath Oysters is still a small and artisanal business, with a team of three, producing around 150,000 oysters each year. The plan is to produce 400,000 oysters each year, using old-fashioned methods.

Patrick and Lucy point out that there are few more sustainable protein and nutrient-rich foods than oysters because, as filter feeders, they thrive at the base of food chains. They eat single-celled algae and other tiny organic particles that are naturally present in seawater. These algae are our planet's main synthesisers of omega-3 oils, making oysters a rich source of essential nutrients, comparable in levels to some oily fish that live much higher up food chains. They are also rich in vitamin B12 and a source of vitamin D.

However, they also admit that every oyster farm and its produce is different, each influenced by the balance of sea and fresh water, the foods available to the oysters, the water chemistry, temperature, site characteristics and the weather. In essence, the taste of an oyster varies according to where it is grown – its *terroir* – just like wine. So, the wild environment and harsh climate of the Kyle of Durness and Cape Wrath impart Cape Wrath Oysters with their own distinctive characteristics and sweet, briny flavour.

To savour a Cape Wrath Oyster, Patrick and Lucy suggest chewing it a couple of times to expand the flavours in your mouth and pay due respect to the oyster. They are plump, sweet and creamy and an ultimate nutritious treat. A squeeze of lemon enhances the flavour of the oyster, keeping the purity of the taste. A drop of Tabasco lifts the flavour and enhances the texture, and a traditional *mignonette* of finely diced shallots, red wine vinegar and cracked black peppercorns accentuates the texture and the flavour.

Cape Wrath Oysters Mombasa

Serves 3–4

roughly 12 fresh Cape Wrath oysters, shucked, patted dry and placed on the deeper half shell

1 tbsp ghee

2 plump garlic cloves, finely chopped

1 tsp cumin seeds

1 tsp jaggery or muscovado sugar

1–2 tsp harissa paste, or a hot chilli sauce of your choice

2 tbsp tomato paste

a bunch of fresh coriander, finely chopped (reserve some for garnishing)

300ml white wine

sea salt

Oysters Mombasa are simply oysters baked in a hot sauce – a popular dish around the Indian Ocean that will please all the chilli lovers of the Atlantic Ocean and the North Sea – but I thought the recipe would bring together the African connection of Patrick and Lucy Blow with their oyster farm in the Scottish Highlands.

Preheat the oven to 180°C (fan 160°C), 350°F, gas mark 4.

Arrange the oysters in their half shells on a baking dish.
Melt the ghee in a heavy-based saucepan and stir in the garlic and cumin seeds, until fragrant. Stir in the jaggery and when it melts add the harissa, tomato paste and coriander.

Pour in the wine and bring the sauce to the boil, stirring to make sure it is blended, and season with salt.

Spoon a little of the sauce over each oyster and place them in the oven for about 8 minutes.

Sprinkle the reserved coriander over the baked oysters and serve the leftover sauce on the side.

Cape Wrath Oysters with Cream and Parmesan

Not everyone enjoys the thought and texture of a raw oyster but a simply cooked one with Parmesan and cream often goes down a treat. If you haven't eaten or cooked oysters before this is a good recipe to start with. Serve them as a hot canapé, or as simple meal with a salad, and finish them with a few drops of Worcester sauce, Tabasco or sriracha, if you like.

Preheat the grill to high.

Melt the butter in a saucepan and pour it into the deeper half shell. Place the oysters on top of the butter in their shells on a baking tray. Drizzle a teaspoonful of cream over each one, season with black pepper and sprinkle generously with the Parmesan.

Pop the oysters under the grill for roughly a minute, until the cheese browns.

Serve immediately with a sprinkling of parsley and with a drop of Worcestershire or hot sauce, if you like.

Serves 4 (or 20 canapés)

———

50 g butter

20 Cape Wrath oysters, shucked, drained of liquid and kept in the deeper half shell

double cream

freshly ground black pepper

50g Parmesan, finely grated

1 tbsp parsley, finely chopped

Lea & Perrins Worcestershire sauce, Tabasco, sriracha, to finish

Shore Seaweed's Ramen Broth with Five Spice Fish Balls

The shoreline between Castle of Mey and Wick is a good area for high-water exchange and rock shelving, perfect conditions for nutrient-dense seaweed to thrive. When Shore Seaweed recognised this superfood right on its doorstep in 2016 it obtained a licence to cover 17 species along 56 kilometres of the shoreline. The seaweed harvesters stick to the lunar pattern and select nine of those species in peak condition, trimming by hand so that they leave a substantial stalk behind to enable natural regrowth. It is these sustainable and low-environmental-impact practices that Shore Seaweed prides itself on, and the recognised health properties of the plant have inspired the company to turn local seaweed into everyday snacks and foods,

Serves 4

———

For the fish balls

450g fresh white fish fillets (haddock, cod, whiting, bream), boned and flaked

1–2 tsp Chinese five spice

sea salt and freshly ground black pepper

4 tbsp water

3–4 tbsp rice flour

1.5 litres seaweed ramen broth

1–2 tbsp naturally brewed soy sauce

a handful of kale leaves, shredded

200g fresh rice noodles, or 100g dried rice noodles, soaked in hot water until soft

2 spring onions, trimmed and finely sliced

1 red or green chilli, stalk and seeds removed, and finely sliced

a small bunch of fresh coriander, finely chopped

Shore Seeweed harvesters on Scotland's north-east coast.

the latest product being a delicious ramen broth made with seaweed, which I have used in this recipe.

To make the fish balls, pound the flaked flesh to a paste, using a mortar and pestle. Add the spice and season with salt and pepper. Add the water and mix in enough rice flour to form a paste-like texture. Dampen your hands and pick up a small portion of the fish mixture, squeezing it to form a cherry-sized ball. Do the same with the rest of the mixture.

Meanwhile, bring the seaweed ramen broth to the boil in a deep pot and season it to your taste with soy sauce. Drop in the fish balls and simmer for about 5 minutes. Add the shredded kale and cook for a minute.

Divide the noodles amongst four bowls. Using a slotted spoon, add the fish balls and kale to the noodles, then ladle the hot ramen broth over the top. Garnish with the spring onions and chilli and sprinkle with the chopped coriander.

Keltic Seafare Scotland (Dingwall)

Alasdair Hughson's favourite places to fish are the Sound of Mull and the pristine tidal waters around Jura, Harris, the Uists and the north-west coast. He says he's not so keen on Mallaig as it is very exposed to the south-west winds and there are so many prawn trawlers going in and out of the harbour at funny hours of the night that it is difficult to get any sleep. Not something most of us think about in a fisherman's life.

Alasdair grew up loving life on a boat. He has fond memories of spending time with his father, Eddie, in a caravan at Loch Eriboll in the very north of Scotland when he was around ten or eleven years old and would accompany his father on his boat while he was diving for scallops. At that time, his father worked on the rigs at Nigg on the north-east coast and would go scallop diving every moment he could until he was able to do it full-time in 1986, selling his catch to Laurence and Marian Watkins who had just set up a company called Keltic Seafare. Eddie joined them in 1992 as chief fisherman and together they took the company forwards as Keltic Seafare Scotland. Eddie's skills as a scallop diver were fundamental to its rapid growth, from the humble beginnings of a car, trailer and second-hand fax machine to a global business. Once the company started to send the fresh catch on the sleeper trains to London, selling live scallops to the Ritz and the Savoy, to Billy Drabble of St James's Hotel and Club in Mayfair and to Hugh Fearnley-Whittingstall at the River Café, and got the attention of celebrity chefs Jamie Oliver and Gordon Ramsay, its reputation for top quality was cemented.

In 2003 Keltic Seafare Scotland suffered a tragic blow when Eddie Hughson died. He had faced many challenges and dangers out at sea but, ironically, he was killed in a road accident. Alasdair at this point was a constable in the Northern Constabulary but the tragic and sudden loss of his father left him with a dilemma: to follow his heart and keep his father's business alive after all the energy he had put into it, or remain with the police force and the secure income and lifestyle it offered. Alasdair went with his heart.

By 2005 the reputation of Keltic Seafare Scotland had spread and, in addition to the hand-dived scallops, it started supplying live lobsters and crabs and, eventually, langoustines. But, in order to keep growing, the company had to look at new markets and methods of transporting live shellfish greater distances and made inroads into France and Spain. Today it works with more than 100 fishermen up and down the west coast of Scotland and as far north as Orkney, and Alasdair is one of them. He is also the director of the company and chair of the Scottish Creel Fishermen's Federation.

Alasdair finds the recent raft of legislation frustrating, such as the Health and Safety Executive (HSE) rule that every scallop-diving boat must have a supervisor, a diver and a standby diver. These positions require experience and qualifications that very few people possess, making it difficult to build the required crew, but the consequences for ignoring these rules are too huge to contemplate so many fishing boats have gone out of business. 'Respect the fishermen' his late father would always say and these words are at the root of Alasdair's ethos, but the constant changes in legislation make it difficult and suck out all the fun.

With such rapid global expansion, finding buyers has never been a problem for Keltic Seafare Scotland but finding good divers and creelers and holding on to them is more challenging. Alasdair tries to work a four-day week on the boat – Monday to Thursday – with Friday in the factory in Dingwall and the weekend spent with his family in Strathpeffer. He encourages his crew to do the same. The strength of the company lies in its sustainable sourcing from Grade A waters (p.80) off the north-west Highlands and islands, and the careful handling and packaging of live shellfish, transporting them thousands of miles, knowing they will still be live and fresh when they reach their destinations. Currently, langoustines are its best-selling product and, after meeting the 'prawn' fishermen, Heddle (p.106), Josh (p.101) and Louis on *Netta* (p.111) in Ullapool, you can follow the journey from source to factory as the langoustines make their way from west to east in Mark Renwick's white Keltic Seafare Scotland van.

Highland Bouillabaisse

There are some dishes that always taste best in their natural habitat, such as paella in Spain, jambalaya in New Orleans and Cullen skink in Scotland. Bouillabaisse falls into this category too, as it is a traditional, garlic-laden fisherman's broth in Marseille. It is also a dish of poverty – a potato and fish broth served with bread – similar to the traditional Scottish broths often served with oatcakes. This is a great dish for experimenting with fish you might not have tried before, perhaps gurnard or pollock, and you can add spineys (squat lobster) and velvet crab if you can get some. Provençal etiquette calls for bouillabaisse to be accompanied by a toasted baguette rubbed with garlic, or fried in garlic butter, along with aioli (p.8) and also rouille, which is a fiery, garlicky bread sauce (like a chilli skordalia), and served with a chilled rosé.

Serves 6

———

3 tbsp olive oil

2 large onions, finely chopped

2 leeks, finely chopped

6 garlic cloves, crushed

2 tsp fennel seeds

1 × 400g tin plum tomatoes, drained of juice

a fingerful of saffron fronds

a few sprigs of thyme

1–2 dried red chillies left whole (optional)

4 good-sized potatoes, peeled and quartered

roughly 2.5 litres boiling water

2–2.5kg mixed firm-fleshed fish, cut into chunks, shucked scallops and langoustines and mussels in their shells

sea salt and freshly ground black pepper

———

For serving

12 slices of baguette, lightly toasted and rubbed with a garlic clove

a bowl of aioli (see p.8 for recipe)

Heat the olive oil in a deep, wide, heavy-based pot and stir in the onion, leeks, garlic and fennel seeds, until the onions begin to colour. Add the tomatoes, saffron and thyme, using your wooden spoon to break up the tomatoes. Toss in the chillies, if using, and potatoes and pour in the boiling water.

Keep the broth boiling vigorously for 5 minutes to thicken it. Drop in the fish and shellfish, starting with the biggest and thickest – large langoustines need about 5 minutes but spineys only need 1 minute – most chunks of fish need 2–3 minutes.

Lift the fish, shellfish and potatoes out of the broth with a slotted spoon and place them in a heated dish. Keep the broth boiling while you remove any skin or large bones from the fish and separate the langoustine and spiney tails. Season the broth to taste, spoon a little over the fish and potatoes and pour the rest into a tureen.

Dip your toasted bread into the broth and enjoy the fish, shellfish and potatoes with the aioli.

Roasted Turbot Pilaki

Serves 4–6

---

3 tbsp olive oil

30g butter

2–3 garlic cloves, finely chopped

2 tsp fennel seeds

1 tsp caraway seeds

2–3 medium-sized waxy potatoes, peeled and diced

½ celeriac, peeled and diced

½ suede or turnip, peeled and diced

2 large carrots, peeled and diced

300ml white wine

sea salt and freshly ground black pepper

several sprigs of thyme, rosemary or hyssop

1 whole turbot (roughly 1.2–1.5kg), gutted and cleaned

1 lemon, halved lengthways and then cut into thin slices

sea salt

In Turkey, pilaki refers to a dish cooked in lots of olive oil with chopped vegetables, such as mussels in a stew or a whole mackerel roasted on a bed of vegetables. Roasting a whole turbot this way is very simple and satisfying, enhancing the delicate texture of this flat fish. My local fishmonger, Pro Fish Scotland (p.vii), gets turbot from the Peterhead or Shetland markets, usually caught in the waters off the north-east or around Orkney and Shetland, and weighing between 1.2kg and 1.5kg. This turbot is the most conveniently shaped fish to fit perfectly into my roasting tin.

Preheat the oven to 180°C (fan 160°C), 350°F, gas mark 4.

Heat 2 tablespoons of the olive oil with the half the butter in a heavy-based pan and toss in the garlic, fennel and caraway seeds for a minute. Toss in all the chopped vegetables for 2–3 minutes and add half the wine. Keep tossing for another minute to start the softening process, then season with salt and pepper.

Tip the diced vegetables into a roasting dish or tin – I use an old one lined with foil – and spread them out evenly. Scatter a few sprigs of thyme over them, place the turbot on top, drizzle the remaining tablespoon of oil over the fish and pour in the rest of the wine. Arrange the slices of lemon over the skin of fish, dot with the rest of the butter and sprinkle generously with sea salt.

Pop the dish into the oven to roast for about 25–30 minutes. Serve hot, or at room temperature, with extra wedges of lemon, if you like, and a plain or flavoured mayonnaise of your choice.

The Redshank's Fish and Chips

Driving south over the Kessock Bridge just outside Inverness, on my way to Moray, I could almost smell the freshly prepared takeaway food on the shore below, where the Redshank team, Jamie and Ann Marie Ross, serve restaurant-quality food with a street-food twist. Jamie's father was a prawn fisherman in Kylesku over on the west coast, so he grew up around seafood and loves using fresh fish from Peterhead and scallops from Shetland in the Redshank's dishes. The takeaway business started off with one little trailer that moved to different pitches around Inverness but now operates seasonally from a static street kitchen near the marina, not far from the bridge. As the demand for their seafood dishes grows, so does the queue, particularly for their deliciously fresh fish and chips served with homemade tartare sauce or mushy peas. Here, they've shared their recipe for their beer batter and the best chips, made with Rooster potatoes, which, ideally, you should soak in salted water overnight.

———

To make the tartare sauce, finely chop the capers and gherkins together, then strain off the excess vinegar. Combine with the mayonnaise and add salt and pepper to taste. You can make this ahead of time and keep chilled until ready to use.

Mix all the batter ingredients together until smooth. (The batter is best used within 15 minutes of making it.)

Heat up your fryer to 140°C. Drain your soaked, chipped potatoes and pat dry with a clean towel. Lower them in to the fryer and cook for about 4 minutes, then turn up your fryer to 180°C and cook the chips until golden brown and fluffy inside. Drain the chips and keep warm.

Make sure the temperature of the deep fat fryer is still at 180°C. Flour the fillets of fish on both sides. Dip them into the batter – shaking off any excess batter mix without exposing the flesh – and carefully lower them into the fryer, moving the fillet away from you, so that you don't get splashed by the oil. The fish usually take about 7–9 minutes depending on the thickness of the fillets.

Whilst still lovely and hot, serve the fish and chips with the tartare sauce and lemon wedges. Add malt vinegar and mushy or garden peas, if you like.

•   •   •

Alternatively, you can shallow fry the battered fish in a pan with at least 3 inches of oil at 180°C but make sure you turn your fish for 3–4 minutes on each side.

Fish and chips for 4

———

500g Rooster potatoes, peeled, washed, cut into your desired chip thickness and soaked in lightly salted water for 2–3 hours, or overnight if possible.

For the tartare sauce

30g capers

30g gherkins

240g mayonnaise

a pinch of sea salt and freshly ground black pepper to taste

———

For the batter

140g plain flour

140g cornflour

330ml cold beer (good quality local beer)

1 tsp sea salt

a pinch of ground white pepper

a pinch of ground turmeric

———

4 fresh, skinless haddock fillets

plain flour, for coating

vegetable oil, for frying

large lemon wedges, for serving

malt vinegar, for splashing

4
Orkney and Shetland

The history of these two groups of islands is fascinating in itself, the landscape of one is in complete contrast to the other, and the seafood of both is world class. As the boats followed the shoals, their harbours grew in prosperity during the herring boom but the clean, tidal waters of the North Sea and the Atlantic continue to provide rich grounds for pelagic fishermen with large quotas of monkfish, halibut, cod, haddock, ling, plaice, pollock, herring, mackerel and lemon sole. They provide havens for shellfish too. More than a quarter of UK's fish is landed in Shetland and the relatively new markets in Lerwick and Scalloway are bustling, as are the Orkney fishmongers. Orkney is known for its shellfish, particularly scallops and crabs, and Shetland is the biggest mussel producer in the UK and the provider of a quarter of farmed Scottish salmon.

Jolly's of Orkney (Kirkwall)

On the ferry from Scrabster on the Scottish mainland to Stromness in Orkney, I thought about the experimental Neolithic boat that Patrick McGlinchey (p.xv) constructed out of five cow skins in 2017 for the BBC series *Britain's Ancient Capital: Secrets of Orkney*. Remarkably, it carried nine people 30 miles across this deadly stretch of tidal waters to prove that early Neolithic people were capable of travelling between mainland Scotland and the Orkney Isles. This stretch of water is also the fishing grounds for shoals of herring, mackerel, haddock, cod and monkfish that are landed at Scrabster as Orkney no longer has a substantial fishing fleet.

At one time there were 12 fishing boats, George Stout, the owner of Jolly's of Orkney, told me. So, even though the fish has been caught in waters around Orkney, he has to get his white fish from Scrabster or Shetland. His fresh salmon, which he says is in beautiful condition, comes from Cooke Aquaculture pens, the crabs and crabmeat are sourced locally from Westray or the Orkney Fisherman's Society, and most of the scallops and lobsters come from QA Shellfish owned by Heddle Costie (p.106).

Jolly's of Orkney was founded almost 60 years ago and gained its far-reaching reputation as a family-run, premium-quality fish and shellfish supplier under Billy Jolly (p.135) and his father, but George and Anne Stout have owned it for the last seven years. They have kept the 'Jolly' name because it had become an institution on the Orcadian culinary landscape and when they first took over the business George and Anne would invite Billy to come and cook fish over a gas stove and chat with the customers. They also make sure that they maintain the quality of locally sourced fish and the traditional methods of preserving it. All the smoking, drying and salting are done on the premises and all the fillets of smoked salmon are hand-sliced. Whilst replicating the quality and traditions of Jolly's, George is proud to give it a modern twist.

The main shop is in Hatston where, along with 11 staff, George continues with the hot sellers – the freshly prepared takeaway sandwiches that Billy Jolly started producing for the workers in the area – and he sells frozen ready-made meals using their fish, as well as fillets of frozen fish, and frozen squid sacs and shellfish. The main

shop also sells lots of lemon sole and hake, their own hot- and cold-smoked salmon, smoked trout and smoked haddock, and I was delighted to see they that they salt their herring, ling and cod in the drying room. George and Anne have added a wide selection of deli products, such as cured herring, smoked mussels, fish and meat pâtés, local cheeses, chutneys and farm vegetables, and a more recent venture is the Brig Larder, their lavishly kitted out deli in Kirkwall, which is run by their youngest son, Ben. So, Jolly's of Orkney remains an institution and is well worth visiting for the packets of traditionally cured and expertly sliced smoked salmon before getting back on the ferry to the mainland.

Jolly's Salt Cod Baked with Potatoes and Olives

Inspired by the traditional Portuguese bacalhau, this is an easy and delicious way to enjoy Jolly's of Orkney's salt cod or salt ling. Some recipes call for the eggs to be lightly scrambled through the fish and potatoes, others layer the potatoes and fish with the olives and hard-boiled eggs, but in this recipe the cod and potatoes are baked with the olives in an egg custard at the end. You can ask your fishmonger to skin and bone the salt cod fillets for you.

Preheat the oven to 180°C (fan 160°C), 350°F, gas mark 4.

Rinse and drain the salt cod and flake it with your fingers.

Heat enough oil for deep-frying in a pan or wok, and fry the potato matchsticks until they just begin colour and turn crisp. Drain on kitchen paper.

Heat the oil with the butter in a heavy-based pan and stir in the onions and the garlic, until they begin to colour. Toss in the flaked salt cod and cook for 4–5 minutes. Toss in half the parsley and season to taste.

Arrange the crispy potatoes in the base of an ovenproof dish, spoon the fish and onions in a layer on top and scatter the olives over the surface.

Beat the eggs with the milk, pour the mixture over the dish and pop it in the oven for about 25 minutes, until the egg mixture has set.

Garnish with the rest of the parsley and serve hot from the dish with a tomato salad and chunks of bread.

Serves 4

500g salt cod, skinned, boned and soaked in cold water for 24 hours

sunflower oil, for deep-frying

4 medium-sized waxy potatoes, cut into matchsticks

2 tbsp olive oil

25g butter

2 large onions, finely sliced

4 plump garlic cloves, finely chopped

a bunch of flat-leaf parsley, finely chopped

sea salt and freshly ground black pepper

12–16 kalamata olives, halved and stoned

6 eggs

200ml milk

Jolly's Smoked Salmon Pasta, with Scapa Skiren, Rosemary and Juniper Berries

Serves 4

---

1 tbsp olive, or rapeseed, oil

a knob of butter

1 onion, halved and finely sliced with the grain

2 plump garlic cloves, finely chopped

1 tbsp fresh rosemary, chopped

1 tbsp dried juniper berries, lightly crushed to break them up

approx. 250g slices or offcuts of sustainably reared smoked salmon, cut into thin strips

a very generous dram, or more, Scapa Skiren

300ml double cream

150g Parmesan, finely grated

sea salt and freshly ground black pepper

penne, for 4 moderate servings

This is a quick and simple pasta dish embracing two iconic Scottish products – whisky and smoked salmon – and works beautifully with Scapa Skiren or Highland Park whisky and Jolly's of Orkney's delicious smoked salmon. You don't have to use the prime cuts – enjoy them on Orkney beremeal oatcakes and make this dish with the offcuts.

Heat the oil in a pan with the butter. Stir in the onion and garlic with the rosemary and juniper berries to soften. Toss in the salmon, coating it in the onion and rosemary.

Splash in the whisky, tossing it though the mixture. Add more whisky if you like, then pour in enough cream to form a sauce. Bring to the boil, then reduce the heat and gradually stir in half the Parmesan. Season to taste with salt and pepper.

Bring a pot of water to the boil, toss in some salt, and cook your penne until al dente. Drain the penne and immediately toss through the sauce, making sure it is nicely coated. Serve into bowls and finish with a dusting of grated Parmesan.

Billy Jolly

One of the highlights of my trip to Orkney was meeting Billy Jolly, a born storyteller with a soft Orcadian lilt. Now in his eighties, he took me back to the days when he was young boy walking home from school and would get excited when he saw people in the street holding two or three fish on strings, as this meant his father, a lobster fisherman, was back home. At that time, his father, William Jolly, would leave early in the morning and be back before dark to sell lobsters and haddock.

In 1951 when Billy was around 11 years old, his father opened his first fish shop in a converted coal shed with a modern walk-in fridge and his mother made fish cakes that sold out every time. After school on Mondays and Thursdays, Billy would go around the neighbourhood on his bicycle and knock on doors to take orders for fish, which he would deliver from his little basket on Tuesdays and Fridays. Eventually his father bought him a proper message bike to make the delivery easier and Billy continued this little enterprise until he left school at 14 to go to Lossiemouth. At that time Lossiemouth was still an active fishing port and Billy was sent to the Seagull Factory to learn how to fillet fish.

Even though his father had the fish shop, he carried on fishing for a while in his boat *Marbeth* (named after Billy's two sisters, Margaret and Elizabeth) but then sold the boat to raise enough money to buy a house on Victoria Street in Kirkwall to convert into a new fish shop. It was a three-storey house and he only needed the ground floor for the shop so he sold the top two floors. In order to create the shop and open up one side for a large window, Billy's father had to use the crane from the pier, the only crane on the island, to put in the joists to support the floor above. Named William Jolly, the shop sold fresh, smoked and salted fish, poultry, fruit, vegetables, cheese and a variety of delicatessen goods.

Around that time, local divers had discovered scallops, which they called clams, and asked William Jolly if he could find a market for them. Initially, they were sold in the shop but as the quantities grew they had to look for a bigger market and found one near Pudding Lane in London. Once they had received samples of processed, blast-frozen scallop meat, this London market said it would take everything

William Jolly could produce, so the scallop business took off with sales of one ton of scallop meat a week. Billy and his father faced a tricky problem during the Seamen's Strike in 1966 when the ferries didn't run for four weeks and the scallops built up in the shop. The weekly ton of processed meat had to be stored in freezers until a Hercules cargo plane came over to Orkney and Billy and his father were able to get four and half tons of frozen scallop meat onto it, destined for Aberdeen where the lorries met the plane and whisked the scallop meat down to London.

The east-coast fishing boats, the same ones that called into Lossiemouth, used to come into Stromness with fish. Billy used to see their lights on as they fished off Hoy and then they would steam into harbour before the pubs closed. Billy would meet the boats and get the freshest of the catch and take it down to Victoria Street to fillet for the next day or to smoke in their homemade kiln. When these east-coast boats stopped coming to fish off Orkney – they had become outdated and the new steel trawlers could go out into deeper water – Billy and his father had to source dependable supplies of fish from Shetland and Scrabster. When the Danish and Norwegian industrial trawlers fished in the waters around Orkney, they came into Kirkwall in bad weather. Most of the fish in these industrial trawlers was slung into the bottom of the boat and left to rot as it was to be used for fishmeal but they always kept the 'top of the catch' on ice – some cod, haddock and other prime species – so Billy would buy it and skipper it down to the market in Aberdeen where it commanded top prices.

Eventually, the fish shop premises on Victoria Street became too small for the growing and changing business. The market for blast-frozen scallop meat had faded away as the demand for scallops shipped 'live' to the continent grew, so Billy decided to process crab instead. This required the construction of a new building at Hatston and the installation of a 700-gallon stainless-steel tank which had previously been used as a milk cooler on a dairy farm. With a diesel boiler unit he could boil the water in the tank in 45 minutes and cook 15 stone of partons (crabs) at once by lowering them in baskets.

After several years of processing crabmeat, Billy and his sister, Liz, realised that they were close to retirement age (their father had retired many years before) so they phased out the processing of crabmeat and concentrated on the retail side of the business.

From their shop in Hatston, they sold similar products to the old shop on Victoria Street – fresh fish, their own smoked salmon and local cheeses, but they also added filled rolls, pies and other takeaway products. Billy went around all the work units and offices in the area to take orders and soon they had people queuing outside the door. The biggest seller was the smoked salmon, which received national recognition for its quality and taste. One time, they got an order for 4,300 half-pound packs of smoked salmon for the Cambridge Diet Company to be given as Christmas presents to every agent of the company in the UK. It took Billy a whole afternoon to just cut the strings to tie up the packs; they worked flat out for almost three weeks to fulfil the order and pack it onto a chilled lorry to take down to Cambridge.

Billy and Liz retired in the early 2000s and they sold the Hatston premises; it had two owners before George Stout bought it and proudly adopted the ethos of Billy's original business and reputation and kept hold of the name by establishing the new business as 'Jolly's of Orkney' (p.133).

Westray Scallops in Orkney Cheddar Sauce with Pepper Dulse

Serves 4

For the cheese sauce

50g butter

1½ tbsp flour

300ml milk

200g Orkney cheddar, or other tangy cheddar

sea salt and freshly ground black pepper

sunflower oil, for frying

8 fresh scallops, drained on kitchen paper

4 or 8 scallop shells

2 tsp ground pepper dulse

You could call these 'Scallops au Gratin', 'Scallops Mornay', or simply 'Scallops in a Cheese Sauce' and you can do the same with mussels, prawns or chunks of lobster. I think this was the first way I ever had scallops in my teens – in fact I think almost all the fish dishes I had at the time were either prepared in a cheese sauce, parsley sauce or deep-fried in batter! This is a simple and delicious way to enjoy the Westray scallops from QA Shellfish, which you can choose from the ponds, and if Heddle (p.106) is back in Orkney you might meet him too!

To make the cheese sauce, melt the butter in a heavy-based pan and stir in the flour to form a thick roux. Slowly add the milk, beating all the time with a wooden spoon or balloon whisk, to form a thick smooth, lump-free sauce. Add the cheese, bit by bit, beating in each batch to melt before you add the next. Season to taste.

Wipe a little oil over the base of a frying pan. When it's hot, place the scallops in it and sizzle for a minute on each side so that they are nicely browned and just cooked.

Set your grill to high. Arrange the scallop shells on a baking tray that will fit under your grill and place one or two scallops in each shell. Spoon the cheese sauce generously over them and place them under the hot grill for 8–10 minutes, until the cheese sauce is nicely browned. Serve immediately with a sprinkling of pepper dulse.

'Haddock is not just Haddock' – Dougie Stanger

Dougie Stanger sells the 'freshest fish possible' from his small unit on the edge of Kirkwall. He is in touch with the fishermen daily when they are out at sea. They send photos of the catch to his phone to see what he wants and he will go over on the ferry to meet the boats in Scrabster; sometimes he'll go as far as Peterhead. He is that particular about the fish he supplies.

'Haddock is not just haddock,' he explains. There are different types and different tastes according to the season and location. There are the 'spawnie' haddocks, which follow the spawning herring and gorge on their spawn so they taste completely different. It alters the texture, the flavour and the way the way you cook them. They are soft, rich in flavour and taste like halibut. There are the thin-skinned, sweet-tasting Rockall haddock caught in the waters around the uninhabitable granite islet, a long way west of St Kilda. And there are Faroe haddock, the haddock that Dougie was selling the day I spoke to him, as, due to the fishing restrictions in the North Sea, the fishermen were catching their allocated quota around the Faroe Islands.

Dougie laments that the quota system is crazy. The locals used to eat megrim and hake, now they all want haddock and cod. But there are laws on overfishing cod so, although the fishermen catch cod in their nets all the time, they can't return to the harbour with them so they have to dump them at sea. Dougie has been in the fishing industry a long time and has seen many changes, including the recent loss of two fishing boats, leaving only one in Orkney. He has his own little boat to go out into Scapa Flow to fish for queen scallops but the rest of the time he buys and sells 'the freshest' fish, making it easy for people by selling £10 or £20 bags of fish and delivering to their doors. Some Orcadians are well looked after!

Orkney Crab Linguine

The Orkney Fisherman's Society, established in 1953, is a cooperative so the fishermen have a shareholding in the company and they mainly fish for crab. They fish for them all year round but the peak season is in the last three months of the year when the crab have roe. The processing takes place on the premises and most of the white meat goes to Marks & Spencer to be sold as crabmeat or to use in their products. All the crabmeat from the Orkney Fisherman's Society is labelled 'Orkney Crab' unless the crabs have been sourced from elsewhere.

Crab linguine seems like the perfect dish to make with Orkney crab given that there is a poignant Italian connection through the much-loved Italian Chapel created out of Nissen huts by Italian prisoners of war during the Second World War. These men were brought to Orkney to construct barriers to close off four of the entrances to Scapa Flow after a German submarine sank HMS Royal Oak in 1939.

The classic combination of fresh fennel and chilli works so well with the fresh crabmeat, and you can use linguine or spaghetti.

Serves 4

———

1 whole medium-sized fennel bulb

1 tsp sea salt

linguine for 4 (roughly 400g)

1 tbsp olive oil

25g butter

1 fresh red chilli, deseeded and finely sliced

2 plump garlic cloves, finely chopped

zest and juice of 1 lemon

100ml white wine

1 tbsp crème fraiche

350g fresh crabmeat

sea salt and freshly ground black pepper

extra olive oil, for serving

a small bunch of parsley, finely chopped

finely grated Parmesan, for serving

First trim the fennel bulb of its outer layers and feathery fronds. Finely chop the fronds and put aside. Keep the trimmed layers to add to the linguine water and finely slice the rest.

Bring a pot of water to the boil, drop in the trimmed-off fennel and a generous teaspoon of salt. Add the linguine, making sure it is submerged.

While the linguine cooks, heat the olive oil with the butter and stir in the chilli and garlic for a minute. Add the sliced fennel and cook for 2 minutes to soften a little. Toss in the lemon zest and juice, and add the white wine. Stir in the crème fraiche, then gently toss in the crabmeat and season to taste. If your think the mixture needs a little more creaminess, add a spoonful of the linguine water to it.

Drain the linguine, remove the bits of fennel, and toss the pasta through the crabmeat, making sure it is coated. Divide it amongst bowls, drizzle a little extra olive oil over the top and sprinkle with parsley and reserved fennel fronds. Serve immediately with a dusting of grated Parmesan.

Monkfish Tagine with Cherry Tomatoes and Preserved Lemon

Monkfish may not have the prettiest of faces but it has a deliciously plump, juicy tail, so when I saw several of them in Dougie Stanger's (p.140) unit I instantly felt like making one of my favourite fish tagines. It's so simple and tasty, just requiring some chunks of crusty loaf to mop up the juices and a crispy green salad. You can easily replace the monkfish tail with anther meaty fish, such as halibut, ling, salmon or coley.

First make the chermoula. Using a mortar and pestle, pound the garlic and cumin seeds to a paste with the salt. Stir in the olive oil and lemon juice and then add the chilli, coriander and saffron.

Place the monkfish chunks in a bowl and pour the chermoula over them. Toss gently to make sure the monkfish is coated, then cover and chill for 4–6 hours. About 40 minutes before cooking, take it out of the fridge to remove the chill.

Heat the oil with the butter in a tagine or heavy-based pot. Stir in the cumin seeds, onion and preserved lemon for 1–2 minutes, then pour in the wine and stock with the honey. Bring it to the boil, turn down the heat and simmer to reduce by a third.

Stir in the tomatoes and just as they begin to crinkle, slip in the marinated fish for 2 minutes – you just want to cook the fish through and no more. Season with salt and pepper to taste and garnish with the reserved preserved lemon and chopped coriander. Serve immediately with chunks of bread.

Serves 4

For the chermoula

2 big, plump garlic cloves, roughly chopped

1 tsp cumin seeds

1 tsp sea salt

2 tbsp olive oil

juice of 1 lemon

1 fresh red or green chilli, stalk and seeds removed, finely chopped

a small bunch of fresh coriander, finely chopped

a fingerful of saffron fronds

roughly 900g monkfish tail, cut into large bite-sized chunks

2 tbsp olive oil

a nob of butter

1 tsp cumin seeds

1 onion, finely chopped

rind of 1 small preserved lemon, finely chopped (reserve some for garnishing)

300ml white wine

300ml fish or chicken stock

2 tsp honey

roughly 16 cherry or baby plum tomatoes, plain red or mixed

sea salt and freshly ground black pepper

a small bunch of fresh coriander, finely chopped

Crispy Cod Cheeks with Skordalia

Serves 2–4

For the skordalia

4 garlic cloves

sea salt

2 slices day-old white bread, soaked in a little water

100g ground almonds

125ml olive oil

a dash of white wine vinegar

12 cod cheeks

roughly 3 tbsp plain flour

sea salt and freshly ground black pepper

3 large eggs, beaten

225g panko breadcrumbs

zest of 2 lemons

1 tsp dried oregano

butter or olive oil, for frying

Fried fish or shellfish with garlicky skordalia is a Greek favourite. Prepared with day-old bread, ground almonds and olive oil, skordalia is enjoyed in the same way as Provençal aioli and is very similar to the garlicky bread and nut tarator of Turkey. If you can't get hold of cod cheeks you can use monkfish cheeks, or substitute with fillets of cod, haddock, ling or pollock, cut into large bite-sized pieces. Served with a Greek salad and a glass of crisp white wine, you could take yourself to the Aegean sunshine for a moment.

First make the skordalia. Using a mortar and pestle pound the garlic with a little sea salt to a smooth paste. Squeeze the bread dry in your hand and pound with the garlic. Add the ground almonds and pound once more. Slowly add in the oil – as you would for mayonnaise – so that the mixture becomes light and silky. Sharpen to taste with a little vinegar and season with salt. Tip the skordalia into a bowl and put aside.

Make sure the cod cheeks are patted dry with kitchen towel.

Select three shallow bowls or dishes. Tip the plain flour into the first one and season with salt and pepper, beat the eggs with a fork in the second, and combine the breadcrumbs, lemon zest and oregano in the third.

First, coat the cod cheeks in the flour, then the egg, and finally in the breadcrumb mixture.

Heat the butter or oil in a heavy-based pan and fry the cod cheeks for 2 minutes each side, until crisp and golden brown. Drain on kitchen paper and serve with the skordalia.

144

Rosemary's Crab and Vanilla Soup
(South Ronaldsay)

Serves 4

———

2 dressed crabs, about 225–250g each

1 vanilla pod

25g butter

4 spring onions, trimmed and finely sliced

roughly 200g potatoes, peeled and finely diced

a good pinch of saffron strands

500ml milk

sea salt and freshly ground black pepper

smoked paprika, pul biber, or pimento, for garnishing

When Rosemary Moon, a prolific food writer and whisky apprecia-tor, decided to move to Orkney from Sussex, her friends and colleagues wondered where she would get her ingredients for her recipe writing and blogging. Rosemary had no such concerns. She had visited Orkney several times to write about its aquaculture, and she and her husband, Nick, had been there on holiday so she knew that there was wealth of local produce and two whisky distilleries, Highland Park and Scapa. She also knew that the strong tidal currents around the islands of Orkney provide ideal habitats for the scallops, crabs and lobsters which Orkney is famed for and which are amongst the best in the world. The fresh salmon, farm-raised in these tidal waters, are lean and firm-fleshed, she says, and she has a fisherman friend who brings her mackerel in the season. He has also brought her beautifully sweet pollock caught off the rocks of Hoxa Head in Scapa Flow, and delicious flounders caught a few hundred metres from the Italian Chapel.

In fact, Rosemary is so content with her move to the island of South Ronaldsay, with whisky on her doorstep and seafood straight from the sea, that she has little desire to hop on the ferry in St Margaret's Hope to head to the Scottish mainland. Tucking into the most delicious kedgeree in her kitchen, overlooking the waves and seabirds, I could see why. For this crab recipe, which was inspired by a trip to a vanilla plantation in Kerala, Rosemary has used the local dressed crab for ease and, if you check out her Rosemary Moon YouTube channel for her delightful guided whisky tastings you might pick up a few tips on a whisky to go with it. You can read more about Rosemary, Orkney and whisky on Substack.

———

Scrape the crabmeat from the shells. Pick through the crabmeat and reserve about 2 tablespoons of the chunkier bits to stir into the soup at the end.

Place the shells in a saucepan. Split the vanilla pod with a sharp knife, scrape out all the tiny black vanilla seeds and reserve them, then add the pod to the crab shells with 500ml cold water. Bring to

the boil and simmer, uncovered, for 5 minutes. Drain the liquor and discard the shells and pod.

Melt the butter in a large pan, add the spring onions and cook slowly for 5 minutes until softened but not browned. Add all the crabmeat (except for the reserved bits) to the pan with the vanilla seeds, potato, saffron, milk and reserved shell liquor. Bring to the boil then simmer, uncovered, for 15 minutes, until the potato is cooked.

Cool the soup slightly, then blend it until smooth. Season to taste with salt and pepper, stir in the reserved crabmeat and reheat gently until piping hot.

Serve garnished with a pinch of smoked paprika, pul biber or pimento.

Sweet-cured Herring with Waldorf Salad, Toasted Oats and Rye Bread

I love cured herring and any salad combination with it. I remember when the first Scandinavian restaurant opened in Glasgow in the 1970s, my mother would suggest going there for an 'open sandwich' – usually a pickled herring combination on a piece of rye bread – when we were shopping in town. So, here's my version of that delightful memory which seems at home in Orkney and Shetland.

Tip the apple into a bowl and toss it in the lemon juice. Add the rest of the salad ingredients to the bowl. Beat the dressing ingredients together and add enough to just coat the salad.

Drain the herring and cut into bite-sized pieces. Toast the slices of rye bread, spread them with butter if you like, and arrange the herring and salad on top, alternating in a haphazard fashion. Spoon any leftover dressing on top and sprinkle with the toasted oats.

Serves 2

For the salad

1 apple, cut into long, thin strips

juice of ½ lemon

2 celery stalks, trimmed and thinly sliced

6 ready-to-eat apricots, thinly sliced

1 tbsp sultanas

1 tbsp pumpkin seeds

For the dressing

2 tbsp mayonnaise

2 tbsp Greek yoghurt

zest and juice of 1 lemon

sea salt and freshly ground black pepper

1 × 400g tub of sweet marinated herring, or your own homemade version (see p.116 for recipe)

4 slices rye bread, or pumpernickel, toasted

butter, for spreading (optional)

1 tbsp porridge oats, toasted

The Foveran Lobster with Highland Park and Orkney Cheddar

Makes 1 portion in the restaurant

1 × 750g live lobster, or it could be pre-cooked

50g butter

1 small onion, finely chopped

1 garlic clove, finely chopped

50ml Highland Park whisky

125ml double cream

50g Orkney cheddar, grated

1 tsp Dijon mustard

sea salt and freshly ground black pepper

a small bunch of flat-leaf parsley, finely chopped

25g Parmesan, finely grated

Paul Doull, chef patron of The Foveran, and Roddy Belford make a good chef team. Paul has actually worked there for the majority of his chef career, which began when he was 17 years old. He and his brother bought it in 2000. In a sense, it is home. A restaurant with rooms and a view over Scapa Flow, The Foveran is one of Orkney's special places to eat. And Paul is proud to showcase local produce in its dishes, such as this recipe using shellfish from QA Shellfish, Orkney cheddar and Highland Park whisky. This is the restaurant's recipe for a single portion so if you are cooking for two, three or four, simply increase the quantities per person.

First, boil the lobster for 18–20 minutes, cool and cut in half lengthwise. Crack the claws, remove the tail meat, slice into 2cm chunks and place back in the shell.

Preheat the grill to high.

Melt the butter in a small pan. Stir in the onion and garlic and sauté for 2–3 minutes, until soft but not browned.

Add the whisky and flambé to burn off the alcohol but retain the flavour. Add the cream, half of the cheddar and the mustard. Cook gently for a few minutes, check the seasoning and add a good pinch of chopped parsley.

Place the lobster, shell-side down, on a metal tray and mask the meat with the sauce – you will have some left over – top with the remaining cheddar and Parmesan and place under a hot grill for 4–5 minutes, until the cheese has melted and begun to colour.

Serve immediately. Any juices from the tray can be added to the remaining sauce and served separately.

Marian's Roasted Monkfish Tail with Anchovy Stuffing

Marian Armitage is passionate about Shetland's local produce and has written two books dedicated to it: Shetland Food and Cooking *and* Food Made in Shetland. *After studying domestic science at what is now Queen Margaret University in Edinburgh, she went on to teach food and nutrition to 12–19 year olds for 35 years. Her father's family came from Da Ness in the beautiful south end of Shetland and, from her kitchen window, Marian enjoys the southerly panorama of the Scatness peninsula with fishing boats on the horizon.*

Shetland's ancient fishing heritage still plays a key part in the lives and livelihoods of many locals. In 2021 two new fish markets were opened in Lerwick and Scalloway and, according to Marian, one in five of the working population is employed in the industry. 'On a working day, over 20 demersal or white fish boats land around 23 species, including catfish, tusk, ling and megrim; the pelagic fleet of eight vessels catch mackerel, herring and blue whiting; the inshore fleet of over 100 small boats catch scallops, lobsters, crabs and buckies; one fifth of Scotland's harvested farmed salmon comes from 44 marine sites in the tidal waters around Shetland employing 400 people; and there are nearly 20 sites around Shetland for rope-grown mussels.'

In spite of the variety and abundance, Marian says that haddock and a few other species account for most of local retail sales and the rest of the landed catch is shipped abroad. She hopes her books will help to expand the repertoire of locals and will encourage children to enjoy cooking fish. This dish is one that she makes with her grand-children.

Serves 4

1 monkfish tail, approx. 750g

2 tbsp olive or vegetable oil

sea salt and freshly ground black pepper

2 medium-sized onions, finely chopped

1 big garlic clove, finely chopped

2 slices day-old bread, approximately 50g, ground into breadcrumbs

a handful of fresh parsley, finely chopped

grated rind and juice of 1 lemon

1 tbsp capers, preserved in vinegar or brine, roughly chopped

4 anchovy fillets, preserved in oil

25g salted butter

8 cherry tomatoes, halved

Preheat the oven to 200°C (fan 180°C), 400°F, gas mark 6.

Prepare the monkfish tail by rubbing a dribble of oil over it and seasoning with salt and pepper. Put aside.

Now make the stuffing. Heat the rest of the oil in a pan and stir in the onions and garlic over a medium heat for about 15 minutes, until soft and translucent.

Add the breadcrumbs, parsley, lemon rind, capers and a good grinding of pepper. Stir in the lemon juice and set aside.

Put the monkfish tail on a baking sheet and cut 4 deep slashes in the flesh but don't go right through. Push an anchovy fillet inside each slash and spoon the stuffing mixture on top.

Cut the butter into small pieces and place down the length of the tail and arrange the halved tomatoes over the top.

Place the monkfish tail on the top shelf of the oven for 15 minutes, reduce the heat to 150°C for 5 minutes, then take it out of the oven, cover with greaseproof paper and leave for 15 minutes, during which time the fish will continue to cook slowly. Marian suggests serving with boiled tatties and seasonal greens.

Catalan Monkfish Stew
with Shetland Mussels and Scallops

This Catalan fish stew is often prepared as one-course meal with chunks of bread rubbed with a clove of garlic and dipped into the stew. Alternatively, you could serve it with garlic bread. The plump meaty scallops from Shetland and from Westray in Orkney sit comfortably with the chunks of monkfish.

Heat half the oil and sear the monkfish pieces. Lift them out and put aside. Stir the onion in the pan until softens, add the garlic, thyme and saffron, then stir in the sherry and almonds. Add the tomatoes, fish stock and lemon juice and simmer for 15 minutes. Stir in the paprika and season well with salt and pepper.

Return the monkfish to the pan, followed by the shellfish. Cook gently for 5 minutes, until shellfish is cooked through. Toss in half the parsley and scatter the rest over the stew.

Serve with sherry or white wine and chunks of crusty bread rubbed with garlic, or a thick slice of hot garlic bread to dunk in the stew.

Serves 4

4 tbsp olive oil

roughly 200g monkfish tail, cut into 4 pieces

1 onion, chopped

3 garlic cloves, crushed

fresh thyme sprigs

1 tsp saffron threads

200ml sherry or brandy

4 tbsp ground almonds

2 × 400g tins chopped tomatoes

300ml fish stock

juice of 1 lemon

1–2 tsp sweet or hot paprika

sea salt and freshly ground black pepper

roughly 12 plump Shetland scallops, shucked

8–12 Shetland mussels

a bunch of flat-leaf parsley, chopped

Akshay's Shetland Mussels in South Indian Tomato Rasam

Shetland doesn't seem like an obvious home for someone born and raised in Mumbai and Goa but Akshay Borges has been there for 15 years and loves it. He had completed a degree in hospitality management at Queen Margaret's University in Edinburgh, where he had also taken on part-time jobs in cafés and the Balmoral Hotel and loved the energy of the kitchen so he decided to look for trainee chef jobs. It was the flip of a coin that brought him to Shetland – the toss-up was between a family-run hotel in Scalloway or a high-end restaurant in the south of England – and he has never looked back, partly because of the fresh ingredients and partly because he found love.

Now, Akshay and his partner are opening their home to offer a taste-of-Shetland experience inspired by the flavours and memories of growing up in Mumbai and Goa. Akshay enjoys sourcing local produce from Shetland's farmers and fishermen and chatting to them about their way of life, and he takes delight in the fact that the freshly landed catch is on his plate within a couple of hours. As the Shetland mussels are amongst the best in the world, Akshay has shared with us one of his favourite ways of enjoying them with a touch of South Indian flavour.

Serves 4

1 tbsp vegetable oil

1½ tsp mustard seeds

½ tsp cumin seeds

1 thumb-sized piece of ginger, finely chopped

6 garlic cloves, finely chopped

1 small onion, sliced

½ tsp garam masala

½ tsp ground coriander

¼ tsp ground turmeric

1 fresh red or green mild chilli, stalk and seeds removed and finely sliced

20 dried curry leaves

600g fresh tomatoes, chopped, or 1½ 400g tins chopped tomatoes

1 tsp sea salt

20g red lentils

200ml water

¾ tsp sugar

1kg mussels, rinsed and debearded

a handful of coriander springs, finely chopped

Put a pot on a medium-high heat, add the vegetable oil, mustard seeds and cumin seeds, and cook for a few minutes, mixing occasionally until the mustard seeds start spluttering.

Stir in the ginger, garlic and onion, and keep mixing and until the onions turn translucent. This should take about 5–7 minutes.

Add the garam masala, coriander powder, turmeric, chilli and curry leaves. Cook for another 2 minutes, then stir in the tomato, salt, red lentils, water and sugar. Turn the heat to medium and let it come to a simmer. Put a lid on and cook for 15 minutes until the lentils are cooked.

Add the mussels to the pot and cook for another 5 minutes or until the mussels open up. Make sure to mix it a few times so that all the mussels are covered in sauce. Finally toss in the coriander and serve with chunks of fresh, crusty bread.

Shetland Lemon Sole Ceviche with Ginger Juice and Preserved Lemon

Serves 4 as starter

————

a thumb-sized piece of fresh ginger, peeled and grated

zest and juice of 2 limes

1 tsp sea salt

1 tsp sugar

1 red pepper, deseeded and very finely chopped

2 spring onions, very finely sliced

rind of 1 small preserved lemon, very finely sliced

1 green chilli, deseeded and finely chopped

a handful of fresh mint leaves, finely shredded

a handful of coriander leaves, finely chopped

250g lemon sole fillets, cut into bite-sized cubes

olive oil

a fingerful of mustard cress

When the lemon sole fillets arrive in the Peterhead market from Shetland they move pretty quickly to fishmongers around the country. They are pearly white and delicate-looking and only require the lightest cooking – my preference is lightly fried in a pan with a little butter, wild garlic if it's the season, and a squeeze of lemon juice, salt and pepper.

Lemon sole's delicate flesh also lends itself to ceviche. You can prepare the components of this dish ahead of time but don't mix it all together until the last minute, as you don't want the acid in the ginger and lime juice to cook the fish.

————

Put the grated ginger into a piece of muslin, twist the ends to form a pouch and squeeze out as much juice as you can into a bowl. Stir the salt and sugar into the lime zest and juice until dissolved.

Combine the red pepper, spring onions, preserved lemon and green chilli in a bowl. Toss in half the herbs.

Roughly 2 minutes before serving, toss the pieces of lemon sole in the ginger juice and lime dressing – purely to cure, not to cook!

Using a slotted spoon, lift the lemon sole out of the dressing and divide it between plates or bowls, scattering the pepper, preserved lemon and herb mixture under and over the thin layers. Moisten with a tablespoon of the dressing, drizzle with a little olive oil and garnish with the rest of the herbs and the mustard cress. Serve immediately.

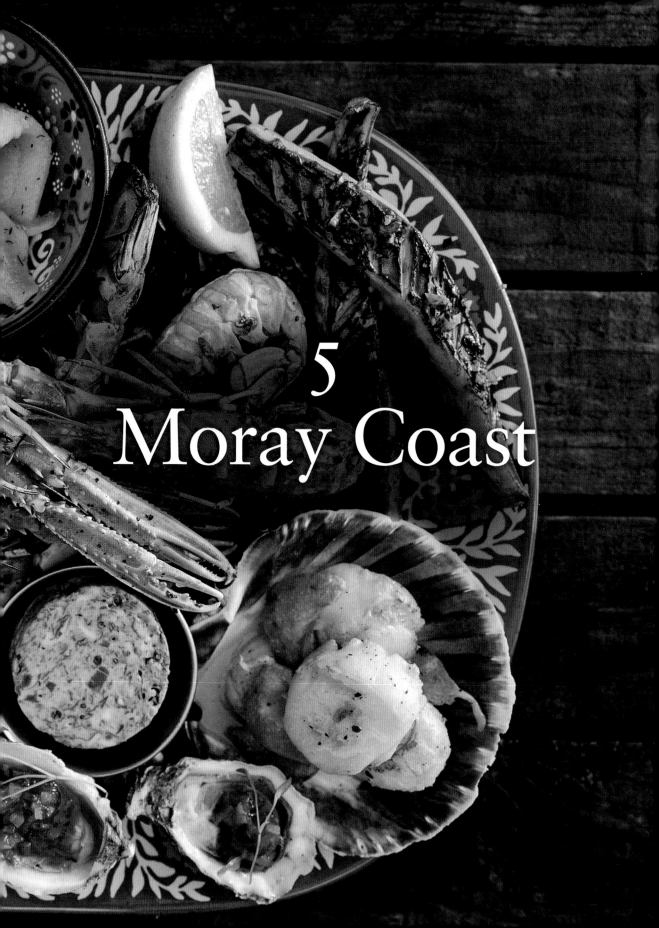

5
Moray Coast

The Moray coast is one of Scotland's hidden gems. There are beautiful beaches and freshly caught seafood sold in fish shops and fish vans that travel great distances into rural areas and over to the west coast. The Moray coast also boasts a rich boat-building and herring heritage – the first Zulu sailing vessel was built in Lossiemouth which, at one time, became the third-largest white-fish landing port in Scotland. Many ports and small fishing villages grew along the coast during the herring boom and some, such as Burghead, Hopeman, Buckie, Findochty, Cullen and Portnockie, still operate as working harbours for small fishing fleets and vessels engaged in shellfish and squid. Moray is also home to the ice house and salmon fishing and processing station at Spey Bey, the famous, smoky broth Cullen skink, and the Fishing Heritage Centre in Buckie, where you can learn about the fishing boats, the fisher wives and herring lassies, and the lives they led.

The Fish Trawler (Elgin)

'The lobster has gone AWOL,' my friend Liz Ashworth said apologetically. 'The fisherman left it in a creel by the harbour late last night for Ian to pick up this morning but it has gone.' A pity, because fresh Moray Firth lobster is much sought after. But Ian McCallion had managed to get everything else we needed for the photo shoot of Martha's Mexican Paella (p.167) – langoustines, mussels, squid, hake – and Arbroath Smokies for her Minilla (p.170), hot-smoked salmon for Liz's Hairy Tatties (p.176) and other seafood required for the dishes we photographed for this book at Bootleggers (p.162) in Hopeman.

If you're doing a bit of DIY in Moray, you will see Ian McCallion's van, The Fish Trawler, in the B&Q car park from Tuesday to Saturday each week. After identifying the need for a reliable outlet selling fresh, quality seafood in Elgin and a site that would provide easy access and free parking, Ian began trading from the car park in 2016. He enjoys sourcing from the local fishermen and fish merchants all the way along the Moray coast to Aberdeen and has built up a sound reputation for his friendly service. During the first pandemic lockdown he was shocked by a radio interview with an exhausted nurse who had come off duty to find no food left in the supermarket so he immediately loaded his van with supplies and parked outside the local hospital to support staff coming off duty. Since the pandemic, The Fish Trawler has thrived. Ian employs three part-time staff and also has a fish van that delivers locally three days a week.

He started experimenting with lightly brined fresh salmon, which he hot-smoked over whisky barrel chips to impart sweetness to the flesh, using the offcuts to make a hot-smoked salmon pâté. Since then he has introduced a wide variety of homemade products to The Fish Trawler, such as salmon kebabs, lemon and pepper haddock and prawn cocktail, and has expanded his fresh seafood to include sea bass, halibut, lemon and grey sole, hake, monkfish tails, haddock, squid, langoustines and scallops from Shetland. Liz, who has known Ian for a long time, says he prides himself in being able to get anything and always the best, including live crabs and lobsters – when they don't escape!

Bootleggers' Crispy Moray Firth Squid with Green Chilli Oil and Roast Garlic Aioli

Serves 4–6

For the roasted garlic aioli

4–6 garlic cloves, crushed (1 clove per person)

olive oil, for drizzling

150g homemade, or shop-bought, mayonnaise

juice of ½ lemon

sea salt

For the green chilli oil

4 fresh green chillies, seeds and stalks removed

1 garlic clove

olive oil

zest and juice of 1 lemon

sea salt and freshly ground black pepper

500g fresh squid tubes and tentacles, rinsed and patted dry

50g plain flour

50g corn flour

1–2 tsp mild chilli powder

1 tsp sea salt

vegetable oil, for deep-frying

1 lemon, cut into wedges, for serving

Bootleggers Bar & Grill in Hopeman has become an exciting foodie hotspot on a beautiful stretch of the Moray coast. Converted out of shipping containers with interesting nautical features, wood-smoked dishes and tapas-style sharing plates, you can watch dolphins and seals out in the water while you tuck into a bowl of plump mussels or crispy fried squid. Most of the fish and shellfish is locally sourced, much of it landed in Hopeman and nearby Burghead – you can sit on the upstairs deck and watch the lobster man hauling his creels out on the bay. With its fresh sea breeze and friendly service, Bootleggers is the recent creation of Barry and Ruthie Scott, an energetic duo who own West Beach Caravan Park on the same stretch of beach and The Bothy Bistro in Burghead where Masterchef judge William Sitwell was so impressed with the food he ranked it in his top 15 restaurants in the UK, describing it in The Telegraph *as 'fresh and exciting because it's not posh'.*

Preheat oven to 200°C (fan 180°C), 400°F, gas mark 6.

First, prepare the aioli. Place the garlic cloves in a piece of tin foil, drizzle with a little olive oil and roast in the oven until soft. Pound the roasted garlic to a paste and combine with the mayonnaise, lemon juice and salt to taste.

For the green chilli oil, whizz the green chillies with the garlic in an electric blender. Gradually add in olive oil until you reach pouring consistency. Pour it into a bowl, stir in the lemon zest and juice and season to taste.

Using a sharp knife, trim the tentacles and slice the tubes into rings roughly 1–2cm thick.

Heat enough oil for deep-frying in a large, heavy-based pan. Combine the flours, chilli powder and salt in a shallow bowl and toss the squid rings and tentacles in it. When the oil is ready for deep-frying (test with a cube of bread), fry the squid in batches for about 2 minutes, until crisp and golden.

Drain on kitchen paper and serve hot with a drizzle of green chilli oil, a wedge of lemon for squeezing and the aioli for dipping.

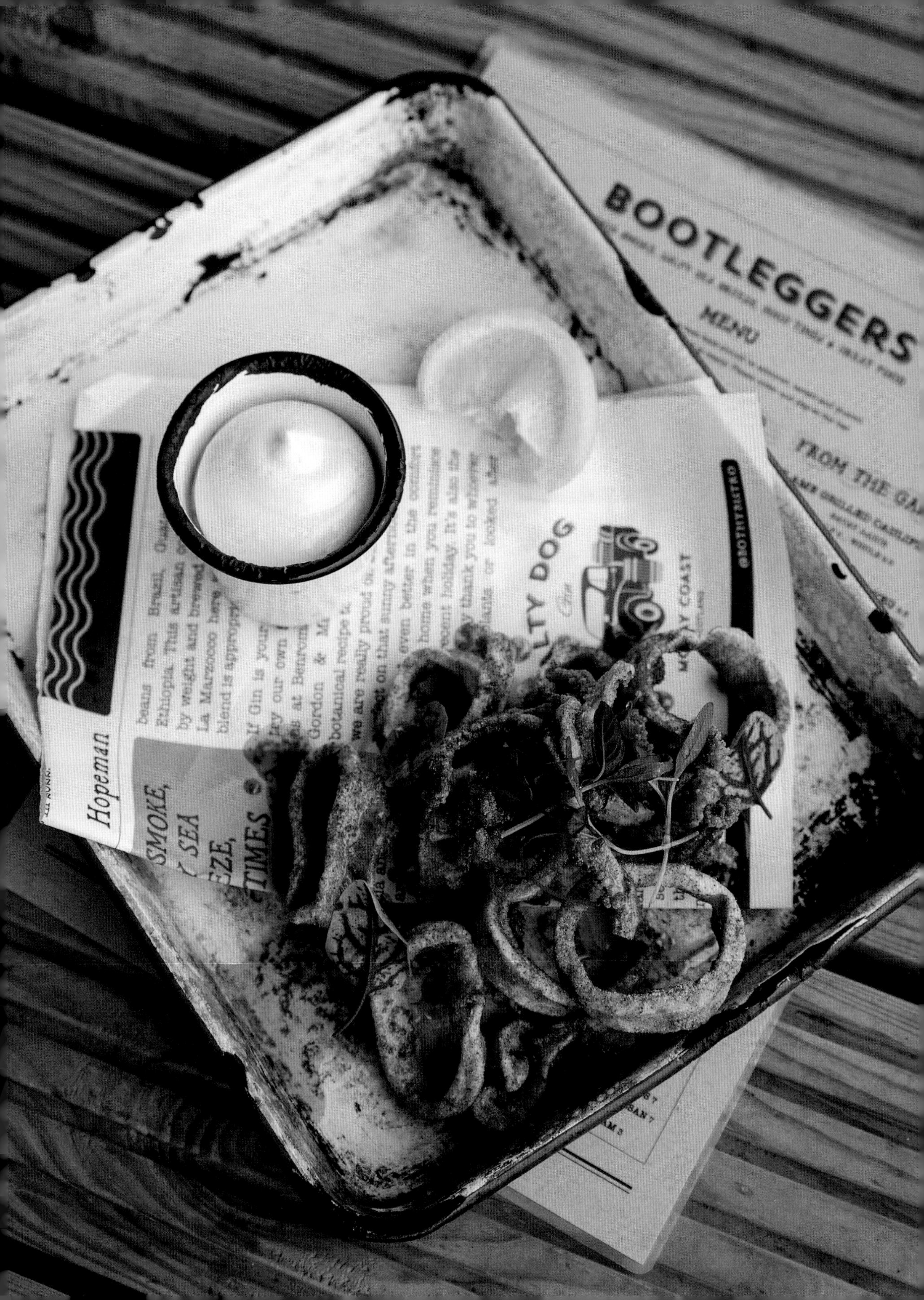
BOOTLEGGERS
MENU
Hopeman

Charred Squid with Tomato and Tamarind Dressing

Serves 4

For the dressing

1 tbsp tamarind paste

juice and zest of 1 lime

2 tbsp fish sauce

1 tbsp jaggery, muscovado sugar or agave syrup

1 clove garlic, crushed

2 shallots, halved and finely chopped

1–2 fresh green or red chillies, stalks and seeds removed, and finely chopped

olive, sunflower or rapeseed oil, for grilling

2 large tomatoes, skinned, deseeded and cut in half

a small bunch of basil leaves

a small bunch of coriander leaves, chopped

a small bunch of mint leaves, chopped

sea salt and freshly ground black pepper

500g fresh baby squid, prepared by your fishmonger, or prepared as above

We ended up with a lot of squid from The Fish Trawler for the photo shoot at Bootleggers so I took some home to make this fresh, summery dish. It is best made with baby squid because they are more tender and sweet.

To prepare the squid, get a firm hold of the head and pull it from the body. Reach down inside the body sac and pull out the transparent backbone, as well as any stringy bits. Rinse the body sac inside and out and pat dry. Cut the tentacles off above the eyes and add to the pile of squid you're going to cook. Discard everything else.

In a bowl, combine the dressing ingredients, mix well and put aside.

Heat up a grill pan, wipe with a little oil, and grill the tomatoes until lightly charred. Transfer them to a board, chop roughly into bite-size chunks, and pop them into a bowl. Add most of the herbs and season with salt and pepper.

Clean the grill, then heat it up again and wipe with a little more oil. Grill the squid for 2–3 minutes each side, pressing them down with a spatula until nicely charred. Transfer the squid to the bowl with the dressing and toss well.

Arrange the tomatoes and herbs on a dish, add the squid and dressing to the dish, garnish with the rest of the herbs and serve while the squid is still warm.

Hake in Tahini Sauce
with Gazpacho Salad

Inspired by the way red mullet is sometimes cooked, or served, with a tahini sauce in Turkey and the Eastern Mediterranean, this recipe works for meaty fillets of fish available from The Fish Trawler (p.161) like hake, halibut, coley or salmon. A crunchy, zesty salad makes a nice contrast to the creamy tahini.

Preheat the oven to 200°C (fan 180°C), 400°F, gas mark 6.

First prepare the salad and the dressing. Heat enough olive to cover the base of a frying pan. Toss in the bread chunks until crispy and golden brown. Drain on kitchen paper and keep aside. Put all the vegetable ingredients into a bowl and keep aside.

For the dressing, use a mortar and pestle to crush the garlic to a paste with the salt, cumin and coriander seeds. Add the oil, vinegar, lemon juice and honey, and season well with pepper. Keep aside.

Pat the hake fillets dry with a kitchen towel. Lightly oil a cast-iron or ovenproof pan, and place it over the heat until hot. Carefully, place the fillets in it, skin-side down, to sizzle and sear for a minute. Drizzle the top with a little oil and place the fillets in the oven for 5 minutes.

Quickly spoon the tahini into a bowl with the garlic and beat in the lemon juice – it will stiffen the mixture so you need to add enough water to thin it down to the consistency of double cream. Season it with salt and pepper.

Take the fillets out of the oven and pour the tahini sauce around them. Return to the oven for another 2–3 minutes to heat through the tahini.

Assemble the salad by layering the fried bread with the chopped vegetables, finishing with bread and the reserved parsley at the top. Pour the dressing over the salad, sprinkle the hake with the toasted sesame seeds and serve together while the hake and tahini are hot.

Serves 4

For the salad

1–2 tbsp olive oil

2 slices day-old bread, broken into small pieces

a handful of cherry or sugar drop tomatoes, halved

a chunk of cucumber, deseeded and finely diced

1 yellow or orange pepper, deseeded and finely diced

1 small red onion, finely chopped

1 fresh green or red chilli, deseeded and finely sliced

a small bunch of flat-leaf parsley, finely chopped (reserve a little for garnishing)

For the dressing

3–4 garlic cloves

sea salt

1 tsp cumin seeds

1 tsp coriander seeds

4 tbsp olive oil

1 tbsp vinegar

juice of 1 lemon

2 tsp honey

freshly ground black pepper

500g hake fillets, skin on

2–3 tbsp olive oil

4 tbsp creamy tahini

2 garlic cloves, crushed

juice of 2 lemons

1 tbsp toasted sesame seeds

Grilled Coley with Anchovy Butter and Pickled Cucumber

Serves 4

For the pickled cucumber

1 cucumber, halved and spiralled into ribbons

1 tsp sea salt

1 tbsp white wine vinegar

1 tbsp caster sugar

For the butter

100g softened butter

1 tbsp anchovy paste

1 tbsp capers in vinegar, drained and finely chopped

juice of ½ lemon

freshly ground black pepper

4 coley fillets, rinsed and patted dry

olive oil

sea salt, to season

You can grill, roast, poach or pan-fry your fish fillets – whichever method you prefer – but it's always handy to have a few simple savoury butters and sauces up your sleeve to serve with them. This is also a great way of experimenting with fish that you might not have cooked before so, instead of the familiar cod, haddock, salmon and trout fillets, you might like to try coley, as I suggest here, or ling, hake, gurnard, sea bass, halibut, herring or mackerel.

Preheat the grill to hot.

Toss the cucumber in a colander with the sea salt and leave to weep for 10–15 minutes. Gently squeeze out any extra moisture and pat dry. Toss the cucumber in a bowl with the vinegar and caster sugar and leave to marinate until ready to use.

Beat the butter in a bowl, then beat in the anchovy paste and capers. Add the lemon juice and season with black pepper.

Rub each fillet with a little olive oil and season with salt. Place the fillets on a baking or grill tray and cook under the grill for roughly 3 minutes each side. Immediately spread the anchovy butter over them and serve while it's melting.

Serve with the pickled cucumber and some boiled new potatoes.

Martha's Mexican Paella

When Martha Doyle first came to Scotland from Veracruz in Mexico, she set the taste buds of Angus on fire in her small, successful restaurant, El Tajin, where she combined local produce with Mexican flavours. Sadly, El Tajin became a casualty of the pandemic lockdowns so Martha is currently based on the Moray coast, where she has added her exciting culinary flair to the sharing menu at Bootleggers (p.162). Back home in Mexico, Martha prepares a seafood rice dish called Arroz a la Tumbada, *cooked in a clay pot and packed full of clams, crabs, octopus, prawns and fish, which remains soupy whereas Spanish paella is cooked until the rice goes crunchy on the bottom, the* socarrat. *So, in her Mexican paella, Martha combines the Spanish and Mexican methods to give you the option of retaining a little liquid in the dish. With a beaming smile big enough to fill the kitchen, she says a tasty paella is all about the sofrito!*

Serves 4–6

For the fish stock (this can be prepared several days in advance)

½ leek

3 celery sticks

3 carrots

1 bay leaves

1 sprig of thyme

1 sprig of thyme

bones, head and all trimmings from fish and prawns

a handful of parsley stalks

sea salt and freshly ground pepper

First, prepare the stock. Put all the ingredients into a stockpot, cover with plenty of water and bring to the boil. Reduce the heat, put on the lid, and simmer for 2 hours. Strain the stock and keep 750ml for the paella.

To prepare the sofrito, heat the oil in a wide, shallow pan. Stir in the garlic and shallots and cook for 2–3 minutes. Add the peppers and cook until soft, then stir in the rest of ingredients, apart from the wine. Reduce the heat and cook gently, until the liquid has reduced. Add half the bottle of wine (keep the other half for cooking the paella) and reduce until the mixture resembles a paste – this will take approximately 1½ hours. Check the seasoning.

Prepare the squid. Using a sharp knife, sever the head and trim the tentacles just above the eyes. With your fingers, pull out the backbone, rinse the sacs inside and out, pat dry and cut into thin pieces. Bring a pot of salted water to a rolling boil, drop in the squid pieces and the tentacles for 1 minute, then drain and refresh under cold water. Keep aside.

Now it's time to assemble the paella. Heat up a paella pan, or the widest, shallow, heavy-based pan you have. Wipe the pan with a little olive oil, roughly 1–2 tsp, and brown the chunks of fish. Transfer them to a plate, or board, to be incorporated later. Tip the sofrito into the pan and bubble it up. Toss in the rice, coating it in the sofrito, add the remaining half bottle of wine and cook gently, until the wine has reduced. Now add the reserved 750ml of fish stock. Give the rice one last stir, making sure it is evenly distributed in the liquid.

Once the liquid begins to bubble, gradually add the prawns and mussels, the squid pieces, the browned chunks of fish and the fresh peas, pressing them down into the rice so that they cook evenly too. As the shellfish cooks, the rice will begin to dry out and you can decide if you want to keep it a little soupy, Mexican-style, or if you want to cook it until you hear the rice crackling as the socarrat forms on the base of the pan.

Serve hot from the pan with lemon wedges to squeeze over it, small bowls of water to clean your fingers from the shellfish, and chunks of bread for mopping up the juices if you have kept your paella a little soupy!

For the sofrito (this can be prepared several days in advance)

3 tbsp olive oil

2 banana shallots, finely chopped

4 garlic cloves, grated

2 bell peppers, red and green, deseeded and finely chopped

2 tbsp hot smoked paprika, or Pimentón de la Vera

1.5kg fresh tomatoes, grated

1 × 400g tin chopped tomatoes

a pinch of saffron fronds

3 sprigs of rosemary

sea salt and freshly ground black pepper

1 bottle of dry, white wine (retain half for the paella)

—

1kg fresh squid

a little olive oil, for browning

1kg hake fillet (or other meaty fish of your choice), cut into chunky pieces

300g arborio rice, rinsed and drained

1kg fresh langoustines, shell and devein half of them

500g mussels

200g fresh green peas

2 lemons, cut into wedges, for serving

Martha's Minilla with Arbroath Smokies

Serves 4–6

_____

12 fat green jalapeños

3 tbsp olive oil

sea salt and freshly ground
black pepper

_____

For the filling

2 tbsp olive oil

2 garlic cloves, grated

½ onion, finely chopped

1 green bell pepper,
deseeded and finely chopped

2 large tomatoes, finely
chopped (keep all the juice)

2 tbsp capers (preserved in
vinegar or brine)

roughly 8 plump green olives,
stoned and finely sliced

2 bay leaves

2 tsp fresh oregano

freshly ground black pepper

2 Arbroath Smokies, flaked
(see preparation instructions)

Minilla Veracruzana is a traditional dish with Spanish roots in the cuisine of Veracruz where my friend, Martha, comes from. The word minilla implies that all the ingredients are chopped very finely which makes it a versatile filling for tacos, tostadas and empanadas, or it can simply be converted into a dip. As a huge supporter of local produce, Martha uses Arbroath Smokies in this dish of stuffed jalapeños, which I have to say, are the most exciting things I have eaten for a long time. You will look at Arbroath Smokies with new eyes!

First, prepare the jalapeños. Using a small, sharp knife make an incision along the centre of each of the jalapeños, slitting them open from head to tail. Gently press from each end to reveal the seeds and scrape them out with the point of your knife, or with a teaspoon. Get the oil very hot in a pan and fry the jalapeños for 1–2 minutes. Sprinkle with the salt and a good grinding of pepper and remove from the pan. This way the jalapeños will remain crunchy with their natural, nutty, spicy flavour.

Heat the oil in a shallow pan. Stir in the garlic, until golden, then add the onion and pepper and cook until the onion is translucent. Stir in the tomatoes and all their juice for a minute, then add the capers, olives, bay leaves, oregano and pepper. Cover the pan, reduce the heat, and simmer for about 8–10 minutes.

Turn off the heat under the onion and tomato mixture and gently fold in the flaked fish. Carefully, spoon the mixture into each jalapeño and serve while still warm.

•   •   •

Preparing the smokies

If the smokies are fresh, possibly even still warm, they are easy to skin and debone but, if they have been sitting on a fish counter for any amount of time, they become firm and more difficult to skin. The easiest way to overcome this is to wrap them in a piece of greaseproof/baking paper and then in aluminium foil and pop them in the oven at 180°C for about 5 minutes. This just enables the flesh to soften a little and separate more easily from the skin.

Lossiemouth Windswept Crab Claws

In the 1900s Lossiemouth was an important port for cargo ships importing goods like coal and timber, and exporting whisky and herring. It attracted many fishing vessels and became the third-largest landing port for white fish in Scotland. It was also where the first Zulu fishing vessel was built – the kind that is being restored at the Johnson and Loftus boatyard (p.114). But now, Lossiemouth is known for its leisure sailing and boating with a modern marina and a long, exposed stretch of beach which might well have inspired the name of the local Windswept Brewery, an award-winning producer of craft beer. So for this Vietnamese method of cooking crab, which involves steaming over beer, then flavouring the broth and drinking it, I have suggested the Windswept Brewery's beers, Lighthouse or Coastal Haze, for their fruity and citrussy notes.

Serves 3–4

———

12 fresh brown crab claws

roughly 600ml Windswept beer, Lighthouse or Coastal Haze

4 spring onions, trimmed and chopped into long pieces

a thumb-sized knob of fresh ginger, peeled and finely sliced

2 green or red Thai chillies, stalk and seeds removed, and finely sliced

3 lemongrass stalks, finely sliced

a bunch of fresh dill fronds, chopped

a bunch of fresh basil leaves, chopped

a bunch of coriander leaves, chopped

2 tbsp fish sauce

juice of 1 lemon

sea salt and freshly ground black pepper

Place one of the crab claws on a board and crack it the middle using the back of a spoon or the blunt side of a chopping knife. Turn it over and do the same on the other side. Pull off the bottom part of the shell so that you are left with the white meat exposed. Rinse and pat dry. Repeat with the rest of the claws.

Pour the beer into the base of a steamer and bring it to the boil. Place the crab claws into the basket of the steamer. Scatter the spring onions, ginger, chillies, lemongrass and herbs over the claws and steam for about 10 minutes.

Lift the claws onto a dish, tip the flavourings into the simmering beer, stir in the fish sauce and lemon juice, and season with salt and pepper. Pour the beer broth into a bowl. Dip the claws into the broth and suck the meat off the claws. Once you've enjoyed the meat from the claws, ladle the rest of the broth into cups to drink.

Opposite: Bootleggers' seafood platter at Hopeman, just along the coast from Lossiemouth.

173

Partan Bree with a
Dash of Benromach

Serves 4

250g cooked white and brown crabmeat

100ml Benromach 10 (or choose a whisky that fits your location)

400ml full-fat milk

50g long grain rice

300ml fish stock, or if you have cooked the crab yourself, use the cooking water

a few drops anchovy essence

200ml cream

sea salt and freshly ground black pepper

1 tbsp snipped fresh chives, or chopped curly parsley, for garnishing

Partan Bree is not traditionally tied to any region but is probably more commonly found in the east and north-east of Scotland. The word partan *is Gaelic and Scots for 'crab' and* bree *is Scots for 'liquid' or 'soup'. The basic dish is traditionally prepared with cooked crabmeat and rice to thicken it and served puréed. A splash of whisky always works a treat in this soup, particularly on a chilly, dreich day. Benromach Distillery, on the Moray coast, produces a whisky range with a subtle, smoky character which is a delightful addition to this soup.*

If you're cooking the soup over a campfire or on the beach with fresh velvet or brown crabs, you might need to improvise – lacking utensils, I have pounded the fresh crab in the simmering liquid and strained it through a sock!

Place the white and brown crabmeat into two separate bowls and splash whisky into both of them. Leave to marinate for about 15 minutes.

Meanwhile bring the milk to scalding point in a heavy-based pot. Stir in the rice and simmer, until the rice is tender but not overcooked.

Liquidise the milk and rice with the marinated brown crabmeat – just the brown – and add a ladleful of the stock. Pour the puréed mixture back into the pot, add the rest of the stock and bring to scalding point again. Add the anchovy essence, the whisky-marinated white crabmeat, the cream and the rest of the whisky. Bring back to scalding point and season generously with salt and pepper – depending on the seasoning of your stock, it will need a fair amount of salt.

Ladle the Bree into bowls, sprinkle with chives or parsley, and serve hot.

Hugh's Hairy Tatties Story

When I asked my friend Liz Ashworth, a food writer, to tell the story of Hairy Tatties for this book, she chatted to Hugh Steven, who was raised on them. Born in 1946 on Overton Farm in Bilbster, Caithness, Hugh has vivid memories of farm life and the amount of work that befell his mother who had her hands full with a household of 11 – his father, four daughters, three sons and his father's parents, both of whom were disabled. Everyone had a job, Hugh explained, milking the cow, cheese and butter making, collecting eggs from the geese, ducks and hens, picking kale and neeps for both the family and the animals, and digging up the potatoes.

They grew Duke of York, Golden Wonder, Pentland Dell and lots of Kerr's Pinks and these, along with the farm milk, butter and cheese, were often exchanged for weekly supplies delivered by 'shop vans', a lifeline in rural areas.

In the height of summer when there were long hours of sunlight, Hugh remembers the salting and drying of the fish in preparation for the winter months. The grocery vans would arrive with whole fish and his mother would brine huge sides of un-skinned, filleted cod and dry them on boards outside the house for up to a week before storing them in the cool of the milk house. Haddock was brined too, and hung over wooden planks, but it took less time to dry and did not taste so salty. Another essential was a barrel of salt herring delivered by the grocer's van from Wick.

The cooking facilities in Hugh's house were basic. There was a small stovetop and few pots so bread was toasted on the end of a fork, scones and oatcakes were baked on a hot girdle, brose and porridge were made for breakfast, and they drank buttermilk. Meals were simple and wholesome, using the produce from the farm and the fish that had been dried, so Hairy Tatties were often prepared in the winter. The salty, dried fish would be soaked overnight in milk then simmered beside a pot of scrubbed tatties. Once the tatties were cooked and drained, his mother would break them up roughly with a knob of butter, mix the hot fish through them and serve with a sprinkling of oatmeal and a homemade oatcake.

Liz's Hairy Tatties with Hot Roast Smoked Salmon and Homemade Oatcakes

Serves 3–4

For the oatcakes (the recipe makes 24)

300g medium oatmeal

1 tsp sea salt

¼ tsp bicarbonate of soda

25ml sunflower or vegetable oil

4 baking trays, lightly oiled

For the Hairy Tatties

450g peeled, floury potatoes cut into small regular chunks

175g hot roast smoked salmon, broken into flakes with your fingers

30g butter, cut into small pieces

sea salt and freshly ground black pepper

If you don't eat all the oatcakes with your Hairy Tatties, store them in an airtight container to enjoy with Smoked Mackerel Pâté (p.55) or Smoked Mussel Pâté (p.41). They are the best oatcakes!

Hairy Tatties were a common staple throughout Scotland and got their name from the fibres of the dried fish, which must have resembled hairs, in the tattie mixture. More recent versions resemble a French brandade, and some even include white wine, but Liz Ashworth reckons the average working Scot was not that sophisticated so she has stuck to the traditional method. Instead of salt cod or haddock, she has used hot roast smoked salmon and serves the Hairy Tatties with her delicious homemade oatcakes, just as Hugh describes. Liz recommends using a floury potato, such as Rooster, Maris Piper or King Edward, but in the summer you can use new potatoes 'boiled in their jackets till the floury flesh bursts forth ready to mix with a knob of butter and flaked fish'.

Preheat the oven to 180°C (fan 160°C), 350°F, gas mark 4.

To make the oatcakes, put the oatmeal, salt and bicarbonate of soda into a bowl. Stir in the oil. Add sufficient water to make a smooth pliable dough and knead well. Divide the dough into four and knead each piece into a round ball. (Oats dry out quickly, so if you find the mixture crumbling, simply return to the mixing bowl and add a little water to bring it together once more.)

Roll out each ball into a thin circle, using oatmeal to prevent sticking, and cut each circle into 6 triangles with a long, flat-bladed knife or baker's cutter.

Lay the triangles flat onto the prepared trays. Bake for 15 to 20 minutes till crisp and beginning to colour. Carefully lift them off the baking trays and leave to cool on a wire rack.

For the Hairy Tatties, simmer the potatoes in salted water till tender, drain well and leave to steam for a few minutes. Break up the potatoes roughly with a fork, add the butter to melt through, and then fold in the flaked salmon. Season with salt and black pepper to taste and serve with the oatcakes.

176

Tugnet Ice House (Spey Bay)

Traditional fishing nets and tools for breaking the ice, an almost intact coracle boat and large boxes used to transport the salmon.

Located at Spey Bay on the Moray Firth, beside the mouth of the River Spey, the Tugnet Ice House was part of the Tugnet salmon fishing station set up on the Gordon Estate in the late eighteenth century. The current structure was built in 1830 – the original one was damaged by a flood in 1829 – and it is the largest surviving ice house in the UK. The salmon would be caught in nets strung across the mouth of the river, then gutted and cleaned and packed in ice in large boxes to be transported by boat to London. The salmon were so large that just one would be packed in each box. The ice would be collected from the winter pools on the banks of the River Spey and deposited through the chute doors high up on the thick stone walls of the subterranean chambers which were cold enough for the ice to remain frozen all year round. The salmon fishing station would have included a fish house, a boiler house, the manager's house and dwellings for 150 workers, but it is the preserved ice house, comprising three turf-covered vaulted stone chambers with a single low-level entrance, that gives us a glimpse of another story in our fishing history.

Kedgeree Risotto with Poached Eggs and Mustard Seed and Fennel Butter

A tasty relic of the Raj in India, kedgeree pops up in British and Indian households in different parts of the world so throughout my life I have enjoyed it cooked in many different ways. At home in Scotland, my favourite way is in the style of a risotto with a good-flavoured stock and the infused milk from the smoked haddock, drizzled with a spiced butter. Cooked in a cast-iron wok, it is moist and spicy, and delicious served with poached eggs, creamy yoghurt and sweet mango chutney – a perfect brunch or supper for a chilly day.

Heat the milk in a wide pan with the onion and spices and simmer for 10 minutes. Place the smoked haddock in the milk and poach gently for about 5 minutes, until it begins to flake. Leave to cool in the milk.

Lift the haddock out of the milk with a slotted spoon, break it up with your fingers into bite-sized pieces and put aside. Strain the milk into a pot.

In a separate pot, heat the stock with the wine and keep it on a low flame beside you while you prepare the risotto.

Heat the ghee in the wok and stir in the cumin and coriander seeds, until fragrant. Add the ginger, garlic, chilli and lime leaves for 1–2 minutes, then toss in the onion and pepper until they begin to soften. Stir in the powdered spices and black cardamom pods with the jaggery and then toss in the rice, making sure it is coated in the spicy mixture.

Stir in one ladle of the hot stock and as the rice begins to absorb it, stir in another ladleful. Gradually add all the stock in this way.

Meanwhile start heating up the flavoured milk and simmer gently. Once all the stock is finished, gradually stir in the flavoured milk, one ladleful at a time.

Check the seasoning of the risotto and carefully fold in the smoked haddock with some of the coriander. Turn off the heat and place a piece of dampened greaseproof paper directly onto the risotto and cover the wok with a lid or a piece of aluminium foil. This keeps the risotto moist and warm while you poach your eggs.

Fill a shallow pan with water and bring it to the boil. Crack the eggs, one by one, into a large spoon or cup. Swirl the water and care-

Serves 4

600ml milk

1 onion, peeled and quartered

6 cloves

4–6 green cardamom pods

4–6 black peppercorns

350g smoked haddock fillets, bones and skin removed

600ml chicken stock

300ml white wine

1 tbsp ghee

2 tsp cumin seeds

2 tsp coriander seeds

a thumb-sized knob of fresh ginger, peeled and finely chopped

2–4 garlic cloves, finely chopped

1 fresh red chilli, deseeded and finely chopped

4 fresh or dried lime leaves

1 onion, finely sliced

1 red pepper, deseeded and finely sliced

1 tbsp garam masala

2 tsp mild curry powder

2 tsp dried turmeric

4 black cardamom pods

1–2 tsp jaggery or muscovado sugar

350g risotto rice (arborio, carnaroli), well rinsed and drained

sea salt and freshly ground black pepper

a small bunch of fresh coriander, finely chopped

4 eggs

For the butter

mustard seeds

fennel seeds

30g butter

For serving

creamy yoghurt

mango chutney, or other
chutney of your choice

fully lower the eggs into it and poach for 3–4 minutes until the whites are set. Remove them from the water with a slotted spoon.

Roast the mustard and fennel seeds in a small, heavy-based frying pan, until the mustard seeds begin to pop all over the pan. Add the butter and let it melt around the seeds until it foams.

Serve the risotto in wide dishes, top each serving with a poached egg and a drizzle of the butter. Garnish with a sprinkling of fresh coriander and serve with a good dollop of creamy yoghurt and chutney of your choice.

Buckie & District Fishing Heritage Centre

Manned entirely by volunteers, the Buckie & District Fishing Heritage Centre is a treasure trove of old fishing photos, black-and-white film footage, books about local fishing vessels, nets, clothing and memorabilia. Here you can learn about the local fishing boats and the remarkable fisher wives who were chosen for their 'brawn not their beauty' as they had to lift their men on their backs to carry them to their boats, and then back again when the men returned from sea so that they didn't get their feet wet.

These hardy women held together their close-knit fishing communities. They would walk an arduous 26-mile round trip to sell their fish in the distillery town of Keith, carrying baskets weighing up to 40lbs. The route has now been restored as the Fishwives Walk from Buckie Harbour to Keith in the hope that people will walk it and reflect on the journey these women made and their remarkable contribution to the fishing heritage of the Moray coast.

The centre also has a stunning stained-glass artwork detailing *The Herring Lassies* at work by Shona McInnes, an artist originally from Orkney but now living in Keith. These women followed the fishing boats clockwise through the summer season from Shetland and down the east coast to Eyemouth, or up the west coast stopping in at important harbours like Ullapool and Stornoway, and some of the women, eager to earn money, travelled all the way from Scotland to Great Yarmouth in East Anglia. By the early 1900s there were around

12,000 Scottish women gutting and preserving herring in different fishing ports.

The volunteers at Buckie & District Fishing Heritage Centre enjoy describing the harsh weather conditions these women often had to endure and how they had to make themselves cotton bandages to protect their hands from the salt in the brine. They worked in teams of three with two processing the fish and third packing them into the barrels. The old film footage shows how speedy and skilled they were, and how they remained cheery, often singing, in spite of their cuts and blisters and the long hours of gruelling work. From 1850 up to the Second World War, 3,000 women from the Western Isles were employed as herring lassies. Their contribution to the fishing industry has been commemorated by the erection of two statues on the harbourside in Stornoway.

Herring in Oatmeal
with Pickled Gooseberries

Serves 2

For the gooseberries

600ml cider or white wine vinegar

450g granulated sugar

pared rind of 1 lemon

a handful of ripened juniper berries

6 allspice berries

850g fresh gooseberries

For the herring

30ml milk

1 egg

25g plain flour

100g porridge oats or fine oatmeal

2 herring, boned, gutted, and filleted or butterflied (your fishmonger will do this for you)

sea salt and freshly ground black pepper

sunflower oil, for frying

1 lemon, halved or quartered

creamed horseradish, for serving

The fish van used to come all the way from Buckie on the Moray coast to my mother's door in Braemar. It was one of the highlights of her week, ever hopeful for dressed crab for lunch, squid to cook in red wine, white fish for a pie and herring to souse, pickle or roll in oatmeal. She would enjoy her oatmeal herring with scrambled eggs and pickled cucumbers (see p.166 for recipe) or pickled gooseberries from the garden for breakfast, but it's also delicious with a tartare potato salad, sauerkraut, or a dab of creamed horseradish and green salad. Pickled gooseberries are delicious and versatile so it's worth making enough to store in a jar.

To make the pickled gooseberries, heat the vinegar with the sugar, lemon rind, juniper and allspice berries. Simmer for 5 minutes, then turn off the heat and stir in the gooseberries. Leave them to cool in the pickling liquid and store in a sterilised jar for at least a week. (You can use them straight away but they will obviously intensify in flavour if you store them for a few weeks, or months – they will keep for up to a year.)

To prepare the herring, beat the egg with the milk in a shallow bowl and tip the flour and oatmeal into two separate shallow bowls. Pat the herring dry and season well with salt and pepper. Dip each butterflied herring into the flour first to coat it, then into the egg and milk, and finally into the oatmeal. Make sure you press the oatmeal onto the herring.

Heat the oil in a wide frying pan and place the herring in skin-side down. Fry for 2 minutes, then turn them over for another 2 minutes, until golden and crispy.

Serve the herring immediately with a dollop of creamed horseradish and pickled gooseberries.

Omelette Arnold Bennett

When I was growing up, my granny always called this dish Finnan Haddie Eggs and she made it with cheddar cheese, but, nowadays, in restaurants and cookery books, it is commonly called Omelette Arnold Bennett after the novelist who had a penchant for the dish at the Savoy Hotel in London where it was created for him. No matter what you call it, the key is the strong smoky flavour of the Finnan Haddie which is traditionally cold-smoked over green wood and peat. The origin of the word 'finnan' has been attributed to both Findon on the Aberdeenshire coast and Findhorn on the Moray coast; if you can't find the traditional Finnan Haddie, you can substitute it with a boldly smoked one from a fishmonger who smokes over peat, such as Andy Race (p.42). Although the dish is referred to as an omelette, it is baked in the oven and more akin to a frittata – perfect with wilted greens in butter, or a crunchy green salad.

Serves 2

roughly 300ml milk

2 bay leaves

4–6 black peppercorns

2 Finnan Haddie, or other good-sized, peat-smoked haddock fillets

freshly ground black pepper

6 large eggs

3–4 tbsp Parmesan, or strong cheddar cheese, grated

25g butter

roughly 3 tbsp double cream

Preheat the oven to 200°C (fan 180°C), 400°F, gas mark 6, or the grill to high.

Pour the milk into a heavy-based frying pan, add the bay leaves and peppercorns and bring it to scalding point. Place the Finnan Haddie in the milk, turn off the heat and leave to cool.

Using your fingers, flake the Finnan Haddie and discard any skin and bones. Keep roughly 200ml of the flavoured milk.

Whisk the eggs together with the flavoured milk and 1 tbsp of the grated Parmesan. Season with black pepper and salt, if you think the fish needs it – often the cure is salty enough.

Melt the butter in a heavy-based frying pan, swirling it around to coat the base and sides, and pour in the eggs. When the base of the omelette begins to set but the surface still remains liquid, scatter the flaked haddock over the top. Pour the cream over the haddock and sprinkle generously with the rest of the Parmesan.

Place the omelette in the oven, or under the hot grill, until beautifully golden brown on top.

Either serve from the pan, or gently slip the whole omelette onto a warmed plate.

Champion Cullen Skink

'Never had I enjoyed such a hearty flavoursome Cullen skink filled with tender meaty haddock. I need search no further. One taste, I knew that it was the best.'

This customer quote comes from a Moray resident who walked the coastal path from Portknockie and popped into Lily's Café in Cullen for a bowl of Cullen skink. As the name suggests, the soup originates from Cullen, a picturesque town that was once a thriving centre for the herring fishing on the Moray coast. It was traditionally made with Finnan Haddie, the local peat-smoked haddock, but there are several modern spins on the soup, some using cream, white wine, stock and herbs. For the local people of Moray, the ones who have grown up with the simple, hearty soup, there is only one way to make Cullen skink – the traditional way – made purely with the ingredients that were available in the fishing towns and rural farms: milk, potatoes, onions and smoked haddock.

I have asked Lynne Watson, the winner of the Cullen Skink Championship in 2018, to share her recipe, which came from her mother. If you would like to dip your spoon into a bowl of Lynne's home-made, award-winning Cullen skink, you can follow in the footsteps of the customer above and pop into Lily's Café, her bright, 14-seater named after her daughter, or try her traditional recipe at home.

Serves 6

1.6kg Maris Piper potatoes, peeled and cut into small and medium-size pieces

1 medium onion, peeled and finely chopped

60g butter

1.2 litres (2 pints) semi skimmed milk

250g undyed smoked haddock fillet

sea salt and freshly ground black pepper

double cream

Put the potatoes into a pot of salted water and boil until tender. Meanwhile, cook the onion in the butter very slowly till it is soft but not coloured. Add the milk and simmer gently, then add the smoked haddock to the simmering milk to cook slowly for 15 to 20 minutes.

Drain the potatoes and add to the fish and milk, breaking the potatoes and fish up with a wooden spoon. Leave to simmer very gently for another 30 minutes, stirring occasionally to prevent sticking.

Season to taste with salt and pepper, stir in a little cream and ladle the skink into warm bowls. Serve while steaming hot with an extra grinding of black pepper.

Seafield Seafoods Cullen Skink Pies

Makes roughly 35 pies, at least 2 per person, so great for a party and they freeze well

---

6 good-sized potatoes, chopped

600g cheddar cheese, grated

a small bunch of parsley, finely chopped

8 smoked haddock fillets

2 lemons, halved

a handful of thyme sprigs

2 litres milk

100g butter

2 onions, finely chopped

2 leeks, trimmed and finely chopped

1.5kg shortcrust pastry block

For the sauce

200g butter

700–800g plain flour

sea salt and freshly ground black pepper

It's quite a big leap from being a beautician to running a fish shop but that is exactly what Gillian Shepherd has done in Cullen. Her husband, Scott, has been a fisherman from the age of 16 and has a 20-metre stern trawler that he fishes out of Scrabster and Ullapool so, in a roundabout way, some of his catch may end up in the shop as most of it comes from the Peterhead market. The oysters in the shop come from Cape Wrath (p.117), the mussels and scallops from Shetland and the lobster and mackerel are provided by local Portsoy fisherman Neil Duguid who goes out in his boat, Emmaley, *named after his daughters Emma and Ashley.*

Gillian doesn't just sell fish and shellfish, she has thought about all the ingredients you might need to go with it, as well as ready-to-cook dishes, smoked pâtés and cures prepared in the kitchen at the back of the shop. There are curries, lasagnes, marinated fish kebabs, stir-fries, fish cakes, a fresh seafood platter that is on a regular order for nearby Glenglassaugh Distillery and the Cullen skink pies that fly out the door!

Preheat oven to 180°C (fan 160°C), 350°F, gas mark 4.

Boil the potatoes in plenty of water until soft and ready to mash. Drain and return to the pot. Add the cheese and parsley, and mash together while the potatoes are still hot.

Place the smoked haddock fillets on a baking dish, add the lemons and thyme and pour the milk over them. Pop the dish in the oven for 20 minutes.

Meanwhile, melt the butter in a pan and stir in the onion and leeks for 2–3 minutes to soften. Turn off the heat.

When the haddock is ready, strain it and reserve the milk. Flake the haddock with your fingers and toss it through the onion and leeks.

Now make the sauce. Melt the butter in a pan, stir in the flour to make a roux and add the haddock-flavoured milk, stirring all the time to make a thick, smooth sauce. Add the leek and haddock mix to the sauce and season with salt and pepper to taste.

Roll out the pastry and use a cutter, or an upturned glass or cup,

to cut out circles. Place them into the lightly greased pockets of a pie tin and fill them with the haddock mixture.

Spoon the mashed potato and cheese mixture into a piping bag and pipe it onto the pies. Bake in the oven for 20 minutes. Serve hot.

Chargrilled Crappit Heids with Black Pudding Skirlie

The old Scots word crap *means 'to stuff', so this dish was simply a fish head, a* heid, *stuffed with oatmeal, chopped fish liver and suet, and then sewn up to seal it before boiling. In the fishing communities in the eighteenth and nineteenth centuries this was often a meal for the fish sellers and packers who couldn't afford the beautiful sides of fish they had just filleted. However, it wasn't always regarded as a dish of poverty and later versions included poaching the head in stock, or adding shellfish and breadcrumbs to the filling. So, whilst trying to keep an element of tradition, I have adapted the recipe to a chargrilled version stuffed with oatmeal and black pudding instead.*

———

Get the fire bowl or barbeque ready.

Melt half the butter in a pan and fry the black pudding slices for 2 minutes each side. Lift them out of the pan, remove the casing and crumble the slices roughly with your fingers onto a plate.

Add the rest of the butter to the pan and stir in the onions for 4–5 minutes, until they begin to brown. Add the oatmeal to soak up the butter and then toss in the crumbled black pudding and the parsley. Season the mixture to taste.

Open the heads wide and fill with the mixture, packing it in. Place the heads on a rack and grill over a fire bowl or barbeque, or a conventional grill if you prefer, until nicely browned or slightly charred.

Serve hot, with sauces or pickles of your choice.

Serves 3–4

———

100g butter

4 slices Aultbea or Stornoway black pudding

2 onions, finely chopped

4 tbsp medium oatmeal

a bunch of fresh parsley, finely chopped

sea salt and freshly ground black pepper

6–8 haddock heads, cleaned and eyes removed, if you prefer

Fish Head Curry

Serves 2

For the spice paste

2 shallots, peeled and roughly chopped

4 plump garlic cloves, peeled and roughly chopped

2 fresh red chillies, deseeded and roughly chopped

2 big thumb-sized pieces of fresh ginger, peeled and chopped

roughly 4–6 fingers of fresh turmeric, roughly chopped

1 tsp sea salt

2 tbsp mild or hot curry powder, depending on how much heat you like

2 tbsp ghee or vegetable oil

2 tsp brown mustard seeds

2 tsp cumin seeds

1 tsp fenugreek seeds

a handful of dried curry leaves

2 tsp jaggery or muscovado sugar

1 heaped tsp tamarind paste

1 tbsp tomato paste

600ml coconut milk

sea salt

2–4 fish heads, depending on size, cleaned, descaled and eyes removed if you prefer

roughly 8 fresh okra, rinsed and kept whole

2 big tomatoes, quartered

juice of 1 lime

a small bunch of fresh coriander, coarsely chopped

4–6 chapattis, homemade or shop-bought, for serving

It's not just Scots fishermen who have included Crappit Heids in their local cuisine – fish heads are sought after in fishing villages of southern India and Malaysia, as well as in Singapore. A big head usually indicates plump, succulent cheeks, which is what you're after. Sea bass, sea bream, sea trout and salmon are good options. Served with chapattis, naans, or sweet brioche to mop up the curry sauce, this makes a great sharing dish. What's more, you will be utilising a part of the fish that usually goes in the bin.

Using a mortar and pestle, pound the shallots, garlic, chillies, ginger and turmeric with the sea salt to form an almost smooth paste. Stir in the curry powder.

Heat the ghee, or oil, in a wok or wide, heavy-based pot. Stir in the mustard, cumin and fenugreek seeds with the curry leaves until the mustard seeds pop. Stir in the spice paste until fragrant, then add the sugar, tamarind and tomato paste. Pour in the coconut milk, stir well, and bring to the boil. Reduce the heat, simmer for 10–15 minutes to allow the flavours to mingle and the liquid to reduce and thicken, then season with salt to taste.

Slip in the fish heads, making sure they are covered in the sauce, and simmer for a further 10 minutes. Gently toss in the okra and tomatoes for the last 2–3 minutes, then squeeze the lime juice over the top and sprinkle with the coriander.

You can eat from the wok, using your fingers to pick the meat and cheeks from the fish heads and suck the juice from the bones and then mop up the sauce and okra with the chapattis, or you can serve the whole curry on a plate with rice and an Indian-style pickle or chutney.

Creamy Fish and Leek Pie

A creamy fish pie can be a very comforting dish, particularly on a cold winter's evening, and it's a great dish for using a variety of fish and shellfish. My mother used spinach in the base of her pie and cracked eggs into it before layering in the fish, covering it with a cheese sauce and topping with mashed potato. Whether you follow her way or mine, you'll have a deliciously moist, creamy pie with lots of mashed potato topping.

Preheat the oven to 200°C (fan 180°C), 400°F, gas mark 6.

Bring the potatoes to the boil in lots of salted water and cook until just tender. Drain and return to the pot. Mash in the butter while still hot, then mash in the cream. Add enough milk to get the fluffy consistency you want and season with salt and pepper.

While your potatoes are boiling you can prepare the leek and fish mixture. Melt the butter in a frying pan and stir in the fennel seeds. Toss in the leeks and cook until they begin to colour. Stir in the mustard and wine for a minute, then stir in the cream. Gradually add most of the Parmesan (keep some for the top) then stir in the chives, lemon zest and juice, and season to taste.

Gently fold in the fish and prawns and transfer the mixture to an ovenproof dish. Spread it out evenly and top with the mashed potato. Scatter the cheddar and reserved Parmesan over the top and bake in the oven for 25–30 minutes, until nicely browned on top.

Serves 4–6

For the potato topping

2kg potatoes (Maris Piper or Rooster), peeled and kept whole

100g butter

200ml double cream

milk

sea salt and freshly ground black pepper

100g butter

2 tsp fennel seeds

3 large leeks, trimmed and finely sliced

1–2 tbsp wholegrain mustard

300ml dry white wine

300ml double cream

200g Parmesan, finely grated

a handful of chives, chopped or snipped

zest and juice of 1 lemon

sea salt and freshly ground black pepper

2–3 medium-sized smoked haddock fillets, cut into bite-sized chunks

250g fresh haddock, cod, coley, ling or salmon fillets, cut into bite-sized chunks

200g fresh, shelled prawns

100g cheddar, finely grated

6
East Coast

Most of Scotland's white fish comes through the markets in Fraserburgh, Peterhead and Aberdeen. The fish might have been landed off the west coast, Orkney or Shetland but it is sold through the east-coast markets to wholesalers and for export. As you follow the coast southwards there are quaint fishing villages all the way to Fife where the summer herring industry thrived in the East Neuk, the eastern corner of the region. Although, there is still mackerel and creel fishing, the East Neuk is perhaps best known for its fish merchants, fish curing and seafood restaurants. The summer herring fishing off East Lothian was important too; some fisher wives would walk with their heavy loads from Dunbar to Edinburgh to sell their fish. When Dunbar's Victoria Harbour opened in 1842, it became a principal port south of the Firth of Forth, berthing up to 600 boats during the herring season, which carried on down the coast to Eyemouth where Scotland's herring industry ended and England's began.

Amity Fish Company (Peterhead)

Born and bred in Peterhead, Jimmy Buchan knew there was only one thing he wanted to do when he left school at 16 in 1976. He had watched local fisherman catch wild salmon with inshore nets and brown crabs and lobsters in their creels, he had seen the big trawlers come into harbour and unload tons of herring and haddock, so as a young boy he knew he wanted to be a fisherman. He also knew he wanted to skipper his own boat. Ten years later he became the skipper of his own fishing trawler, *Amity*, surviving many a storm at sea while out catching white fish for the Peterhead market. *Amity*, meaning 'friendship', was followed by another boat, *Amenna*, in the 1990s and his final boat was *Amity II* on which he starred in BBC's BAFTA-winning series *Trawlermen*. For the last 20 years of his fishing life, Jimmy harvested langoustines but he came ashore in 2016 and started the successful wholesale business, Amity Fish Company, named after the boats that served him so well and where he claims 'nothing slips under the net'.

The fishing industry is part of Jimmy's everyday life and he will never tire of it. He is CEO of the Scottish Seafood Association and is keen to see more young people involved in the industry and also for more fish, such as haddock, ling, whiting, even rock turbot (catfish), to be used in school meals. As a young member of the crew on the white-fish boats out of Peterhead, Jimmy began his career with haddock and, even today, it is the top seller in his shop. In fact, Jimmy's favourite dish is haddock au gratin, prepared with skinless and boneless fillets with a good thick coating of cheese sauce nicely browned under the grill and served with seasonal vegetables. Simple and delicious!

Smoked Haddock Baked
with Rosemary and Chickpeas

Serves 4

———

2 tbsp olive oil

2 onions, halved and sliced

2–3 garlic cloves, finely chopped

4–6 rosemary sprigs, finely chopped

2 × 400g tins chickpeas, rinsed and drained

2 × 400g tins chopped tomatoes, drained of juice

1 tsp sugar, or honey

sea salt and freshly ground pepper

4 smoked haddock fillets, cut into bite-sized chunks

150g Parmesan, finely grated

250ml double cream

Back in the 1990s when I wrote the food pages for the Sunday Herald, *I created this recipe for an article on smoked haddock. It has been a go-to in our house over the years as it is so easy, can be prepared ahead of time and popped in the oven last minute, and if you have good smoky haddock it is very tasty.*

———

Preheat the oven to 200°C (fan 180°C), 400°F, gas mark 6.

Heat the olive oil in a pan and stir in the onions and garlic until they begin to colour. Toss in the rosemary and chickpeas, coating them in the onions, then stir in the tomatoes with the sugar and cook gently for 10 minutes. Season well with salt and pepper and tip the mixture into an ovenproof dish.

Gently fold in the smoked haddock pieces with some of the Parmesan. Pour the cream over the top and finish with a good covering of Parmesan. Pop the dish in the oven for 25–30 minutes, until lightly browned on top.

Serve hot with a green salad and chunks of bread to mop up the smoky, creamy sauce.

Baked Haddock and Miso Parcels

Serves 4

———

4 tbsp white miso

2 tbsp mirin

2 tbsp naturally brewed soy sauce

2 tsp toasted sesame or toasted pumpkin oil

a big thumb-sized piece of ginger, peeled and grated

4 haddock fillets

1 fresh red chilli, deseeded and finely sliced

2 spring onions, finely sliced

a small bunch of fresh coriander, finely chopped

1 lime, cut into 4 wedges, for squeezing

For a quick burst of Japanese flavours, this simple baked dish can be adapted to use any sustainable white fish fillets – whatever your fishmonger has. All the Japanese ingredients are available in most supermarkets. Serve the dish with noodles, rice, potatoes or a simple salad.

———

Preheat the oven to 200°C (fan 180°C), 400°F, gas mark 6.

In a bowl, mix together the miso, mirin, soy sauce and sesame oil. Put the grated ginger into a piece of muslin, twist it into a pouch and squeeze the juice into the bowl.

Place the haddock fillets onto 4 individual pieces of foil, cut large enough to form a parcel around the fish. Spoon half of the miso mixture over each fillet, sprinkle the chillies and spring onions over the top with half the coriander. Pull the sides of the foil over the fish to create a parcel and place the parcels into a baking dish. Pop them in the oven for about 10 minutes.

Unwrap the parcels and serve in the foil with the rest of the miso dressing, the rest of the coriander and limes wedges to squeeze.

Ling with Parsley Sauce

My memories of fish with parsley sauce are similar to my memories of cheese sauce. Whenever we visited older relatives the lunch would invariably consist of fish, usually cod, cooked in one of these sauces. Yet, a freshly made parsley sauce with a seared piece of juicy fish is a very simple and noble dish. You can poach, grill or pan-fry the fish, but if your oven is already on, as you might be serving roast potatoes with it, then you could do a bit of searing and baking. I'm using ling in this recipe but you could use cod, coley, halibut, hake or haddock.

Heat the oven to 200°C (fan 180°C), 400°F, gas mark 6.

Gently heat the milk in a saucepan with the onion, bay leaves and peppercorns to scalding point. Don't let it boil, but keep simmering gently for about 10 minutes.

Melt the butter in a separate saucepan and stir in the flour to make a roux. Gradually add the hot milk to the roux, a ladleful at a time, leaving the flavourings behind. You may have to strain the last ladleful. Add an extra knob of butter and stir in the parsley. Season to taste, turn off the heat and keep warm.

Heat a heavy-based, ovenproof pan, add the oil, and when it's hot place the fish skin-side down in it. Season with salt and pepper and cook for 2–3 minutes. Turn the fish over and place the pan in the oven for 2 minutes. Add a knob of butter to the pan, turn the fish over once more so it is skin-side again and baste it with the melting butter.

Squeeze the lemon over the fish, arrange it on plates and serve with the warm parsley sauce and roast potatoes.

Serves 4

For the sauce

500ml milk

1 small onion, peeled

2 bay leaves

6 peppercorns

50g butter (plus a knob)

50g plain flour

a large handful of curly parsley, finely chopped (keep some for garnishing)

sea salt and freshly ground black pepper

---

1 tbsp rapeseed or sunflower oil

4 pieces of ling (roughly 150g each), with the skin on

sea salt and freshly ground black pepper

another knob of butter

1 lemon, for squeezing

Fish Stew with Dried Limes

Serves 4–6

120g dried tamarind pulp

1–2 tbsp olive oil

1kg meaty white fish fillets, such as hake, ling, coley, cod or salmon, cut into big chunks

1 onion, halved and sliced

3–4 garlic cloves, chopped

40g ginger, peeled and chopped

4 whole dried limes, pierced several times with a skewer or tooth pick

2 tsp ground turmeric

roughly 12 small new potatoes, peeled and left whole

1 × 400g tin plum tomatoes

2 tsp jaggery or muscovado sugar

sea salt and freshly ground black pepper

a bunch of fresh coriander, finely chopped

This style of fish stew originates from the United Arab Emirates, Oman and Yemen, where the small, sour limes grow. They are dried whole to impart a musty, tangy flavour to dishes, particularly fish stews and soups, and they form an integral part of the dish. You can use any fish or shellfish for the stew, and will find whole dried limes or packets of ground dried lime and dried tamarind pulp in Middle Eastern or Indian stores, as well as online.

Put the tamarind pulp in a bowl and pour 350ml boiling water over it. Leave to soak for about 20 minutes. Squeeze the tamarind pulp in your hand to separate the pulp from the seeds and stalks then strain the pulp through a sieve. Reserve the strained pulp and liquid.

Heat the oil in a heavy-based pan and sear the fish chunks for 1–2 minutes on each side then transfer them to a plate. Stir the onion, garlic and ginger into the pan until they begin to colour. Toss in the whole dried limes, rolling them around in the onions and ginger, and stir in the turmeric. Toss in the potatoes, coating them in the turmeric, then stir in the tomatoes along with the tamarind pulp and jaggery. Pour in the tamarind water and bring the liquid to the boil. Reduce the heat, cover the pan, and simmer gently for 10–15 minutes, until the potatoes are tender.

Season with salt and pepper to taste, then slip in the seared fish chunks. Cover the pan again and cook gently for 4–5 minutes, depending on the size of the fish chunks. Toss half the coriander in the stew and garnish with the rest.

Serve hot with chunks of crusty bread.

Johnshaven Lobster Shop Toastie

Johnshaven is home to one of Aberdeenshire's historic fishing harbours – the others are Macduff, Banff, Portsoy, Rosehearty, Stonehaven and Gourdon – and at the beginning of the eighteenth century it was one of the busiest in Scotland. It is still is a vibrant, working harbour and holds an annual Fish Festival celebrating the village's famous shellfish and its prominence in the maritime industry.

Johnshaven is also home to The Lobster Shop, a relatively new and exciting addition to the family-run business, Murray McBay & Co., which has been supplying fresh shellfish all over Europe and the UK for 75 years. The McBays have always welcomed visitors to their Lobster Shed so that visitors can see how the lobsters and crabs, straight off the local creel boats, are handled and processed – even King Charles visited the Lobster Shed when he was the Duke of Rothesay. Three generations of McBays work within the business. Some are responsible for the delicious pâtés and quiches, crab cakes, lobster rolls and lobster salads available to buy in The Lobster Shop. There is even steamed, split and dressed lobster with garlic and herb butter ready for you to take home and pop under the grill, or you could try making this delicious toastie.

Toastie for 1

---

2 slices of your favourite white loaf (The Lobster Shop uses bread from the local Keptie Bakery)

homemade, or shop-bought, garlic-infused olive oil

mascarpone cheese, for spreading

75g freshly steamed and picked lobster meat (from the tail and claw), cut into bite-size chunks

a handful of grated soft mozzarella

smoked paprika, for dusting

Place the two slices of bread on a board, or clean surface, in front of you. Lightly oil the underside of one with the garlic-infused olive oil. Generously spread an even layer of mascarpone cheese on the topside of both slices.

Add the lobster meat to one slice, cover it with the grated mozzarella and place the other slice of bread – mascarpone side down – over the top.

Lightly oil the top of this slice with the garlic-infused olive oil and dust with paprika. Carefully lift the sandwich into your prepared toastie maker and toast it until nicely browned with a good crunch to it.

Arbroath Smokies in Stovies

Serves 2

450g waxy new potatoes

2 Arbroath Smokies, skin and bones removed

30g butter

juice of 1–2 lemons

freshly ground black pepper

In Arbroath's harbour, in the Fit o' the Toon, there are about six smokehouses and fisheries within a stone's throw of each other, all specialising in Arbroath Smokies. M. & M. Spink has perhaps had the most exposure due to Bill Spink, who has carried on the business started by his grandparents in Auchmithie, appearing in numerous press articles and even on TV with Rick Stein. But they all smoke the North Sea haddock in the traditional way – first gutted, the head cut off, salted for half an hour, then hung in pairs with their tails tied by string on rods to hot-smoke over hardwood chips. The skins turn a beautiful coppery-gold and they can be enjoyed warm straight from the fire when the flesh is moist and waxy and parts easily from the bone. Usually you buy them cold from fishmongers and fish vans, so you need to heat them gently to get the flesh moist again and, of course, they are delicious with potatoes in a Smokie version of stovies, a dish traditionally made with leftover beef and beef dripping or gravy. You can make this dish as lemony or buttery as you wish. Serve in the traditional stovies manner with oatcakes and pickled beetroot.

Boil the potatoes in plenty of water until cooked but still firm. Drain and refresh a little under cold water so that they are cool enough to handle but not cold. Keep the skins on, or peel them if you prefer and cut them into thick slices.

Place the smokies in a wide, heavy-based frying pan, trying to keep them intact as much as possible. Pour in a little water – enough to coat the base of the pan – and simmer gently with a lid on to just warm them through. Spoon the potatoes over the smokies, dot generously with butter, pour in the lemon juice and season well with black pepper. Cover and cook gently for 2–3 minutes, until the butter has melted and everything is hot through.

Using a large spoon, gently toss the potatoes through the smokies and serve in bowls with oatcakes and pickled beetroot or pickled cucumber on the side.

David Lowrie Fish Merchants (Fife)

Buying and selling fish is in David Lowrie's family blood. Born and raised in the small fishing village of Pittenweem, in Fife, he grew up looking at the sea, surrounded by folk in the booming fishing trade. His granny ran a fish van and his father was a wholesale fish merchant buying from the Pittenweem market which, at that time, boasted large amounts of haddock and other fish landed daily at its harbour. As a young boy, David was always gutting and packing fish after school and when he was 16 he started working with his father full-time, learning all the tricks of the trade. However, in 1987, when the fishing industry began to decline and boats were forced to venture further out from the coast and had to land their catches in Aberdeen and Peterhead, David bought himself a van and set up David Lowrie Fish Merchants, purchasing filleted haddock to supply fish and chip shops up and down the east coast.

Today, the fish van has gone and Lowrie HQ is a remarkably busy operation located on Netherton Industrial Estate in St Monans. For years, the business used to function from a refrigerated shed but it has gravitated next door to a slightly larger premises with an open shop front and the luxury of a heated office! David's brother, Ed, is in the business with him, managing the shop and the orders for restaurants and fish and chip shops, and his son, Lewis, can be seen walking around with two phones held to his ears as he handles sales.

As there is no longer a fishing harbour or market in Pittenweem, the Lowries select some crabs, lobsters, squid and mackerel from hand-picked local day boats going in and out of some of Fife's fishing harbours, as well as Arbroath and Gourdon further up the east coast, but they source most of the white fish, such as cod, haddock, coley and halibut from Peterhead market, Fraserburgh and Scrabster. They source salmon from the Scottish Salmon Company and most of the lemon sole, monkfish, scallops and mussels come from the Lerwick market in Shetland. I was delighted to see a pile of fresh Islay Oysters (p.22) in the shop's display alongside west-coast langoustines which David regards as 'the best in the world'. These creel-caught langoustines reach the shop via the coast-to-coast 'Scallop Express' run by Andy Richardson (p.206).

With such attention to sourcing the freshest and the best, and with a fleet of ten vans on the road, it is no wonder that the reputation of David Lowrie Fish Merchants travels well beyond their immediate market of Fife, East Lothian and Edinburgh. I'm just amazed they all look so happy and fresh-faced as their busy day begins at 4.30 a.m.!

St Monans Squid with Kalamata Olives and Red Wine

Serves 4

———

2–3 tbsp olive oil

2 red onions, cut in half lengthways and sliced

3–4 plumps garlic cloves, finely chopped

roughly 750g fresh squid, prepared as above, with the sacs cut into thick rings

3–4 tbsp kalamata olives, stoned

2 bay leaves

6 sprigs of fresh thyme

1–2 tsp cinnamon

1–2 tsp sugar

roughly 300ml red wine

sea salt and freshly ground black pepper

a small bunch of flat-leaf parsley, finely chopped

a fingerful of fresh thyme, oregano or marjoram leaves

1 lemon, cut into wedges

This classic Mediterranean way of cooking squid is simple and delicious. Cooked gently in the wine, the squid turns a purplish colour and is tender to bite. All you need to go with it is fresh bread and a salad. To prepare the squid, peel off the thin film of skin, sever the head and trim the tentacles. With your fingers, pull out the backbone and reach down into the sac to remove any mushy bits. Rinse the prepared sac inside and out, and pat dry. Keep the sacs and trimmed heads for cooking, but discard the rest.

———

Heat the oil in a heavy-based pan. Stir in the onions and garlic and cook until they turn golden. Add the squid heads and rings and toss them around the pan for 2–3 minutes, until they begin to colour. Toss in the olives, bay leaves, thyme, cinnamon and sugar, and pour in the wine. Bubble up the liquid, then reduce the heat and cover the pan. Cook the squid gently for 35–40 minutes, until most of the liquid has reduced and the squid is tender.

Season the squid with salt and pepper and toss in the herbs. Serve immediately with chunks of crusty bread to mop up the sauce and wedges of lemon to squeeze over it. Accompany it with a rocket or mixed-leaf salad.

Native Oysters with
Hot Peanut Butter Sauce

This dish is inspired by many from my childhood and travels in Africa where ground peanuts and peanut butter are used in unexpected ways with seafood and vegetables. It is a delicious way to prepare some of the larger, meatier native oysters – perfect with the Islay Oysters (p.22) which David Lowrie sources for his shop. The recipe can be adapted for large scallops and mussels too.

Dry roast the cumin and coriander seeds in a skillet until they emit a nutty aroma and then, using a mortar and pestle, grind them to a powder. Add the garlic, chilli and ginger with the salt to the mortar and pestle and pound to an almost smooth paste.

Heat the ghee in a pan and stir in the onion. Once it begins to colour, stir in the freshly pounded spice paste with the shrimp paste for 2–3 minutes until fragrant. Add the tomatoes, breaking them up with the back of your spoon, and stir in the peanut butter. Cook gently for about 10 minutes to allow the flavours to mingle and for the sauce to thicken.

Meanwhile, mix together the oatmeal, flour and cayenne pepper in a shallow bowl and season with salt. In a separate bowl, whisk the egg whites until light and fluffy. Gently pass each oyster through the egg white and then roll it in the oatmeal and flour mixture until coated.

Heat enough oil in a frying pan or wok to shallow or deep-fry. Check the oil is hot enough by dropping in a small piece of bread to see if sizzles and crispens. Fry the oysters in batches until golden and crispy and drain on kitchen paper.

Quickly season the sauce with salt and pepper and spoon a little into the base of each reserved shell. Place a crispy oyster on top, garnish with the coriander and toasted peanuts and serve with a wedge of lemon. Tip any leftover sauce into a bowl.

The best way to enjoy these oysters is with your fingers. Simply, squeeze the lemon over your oyster, then pick it up and dip into the sauce. Add more sauce to the shell when you need to.

Serves 4

For the sauce

1 tsp cumin seeds

1 tsp coriander seeds

2 plump garlic cloves, roughly chopped

1 fresh red chilli, deseeded and roughly chopped

1 large thumb-sized piece of ginger, peeled and roughly chopped

sea salt

1 tbsp ghee, or peanut or vegetable oil

1 onion, finely chopped

1 tsp shrimp paste

1 tin of plum tomatoes, drained of juice

1 heaped tbsp (more if you want) crunchy peanut butter

---

8 large native oysters, shucked and patted dry (reserve the deeper half shell)

3 tbsp medium oatmeal

1 tbsp wholemeal flour

1 tbsp cayenne pepper

sea salt

2 egg whites

peanut or vegetable oil, for frying

a handful of toasted peanuts, coarsely chopped

a small bunch of fresh coriander, finely chopped

1 lemon, quartered

Andy's Potted Crab

Makes 1 × 500ml jar

———

4 large brown, fresh crab claws,
or 300g crabmeat

150g salted butter

¼ tsp ground allspice

nutmeg, for grating

On his windy hilltop perch in Fife, Andy Richardson has many a tale to tell about his varied life. A poacher in his youth, turned game-keeper for most of his career, he tells stories of setting traps and hunting geese with rich clients. The foot-and-mouth outbreak of 2001 forced Andy to turn from hunting to fishing. He was fixing his Land Rover in a yard by the harbour when an old man approached him to help on his boat. Andy found himself working on an old, stinking boat collecting broken lobster pots and made the grand total of £7! By investing some of his own money in the purchase of Caithness lobster creels, the pair started catching and selling lobsters. And so began a new stage of his life in the fishing industry and the filming of it.

Today, though, Andy runs a busy coast-to-coast supply service, dubbed the 'Scallop Express' as he regularly drives over to Skye to select plump, hand-dived scallops from James Cameron (p.68) for David Lowrie (p.203) and creel-caught langoustines from Bally Philp (p.84) and other creel fishermen. What Andy doesn't know about seafood and how to cook it, I could write on the back of a postage stamp. Throughout his working life he has watched chefs from all over the world prepare the game he has shot, or the fish he has caught, so he has picked up culinary tricks and preserving techniques to get the best out of the products in his pan. This simple, no-fuss recipe is all about the sweet meat of fresh crab.

———

Boil the crab claws in plenty of water for 8 minutes. Crack the claws open and carefully remove all crabmeat. Keep half the meat intact and shred the rest with your fingers. Place the larger intact pieces of crabmeat in the base of the jar and the shredded meat on top. Don't pack it too tightly as you want the butter to surround all of the crabmeat.

Melt the butter, stir in the allspice and leave to cool but don't leave it so long that it solidifies. Pour the cooled butter over the crabmeat until completely covered. Grate a little nutmeg over the top and chill for at least 6 hours (it will last for 2–4 days in fridge).

Enjoy the potted crab spooned onto hot sourdough toast, or take it with you for a wee snack while fishing.

Scallops with Wild Garlic Butter

With the 'Scallop Express' running from east to west and back again, there is no shortage of fresh, juicy scallops in Fife. So this suggestion is with Andy's effort in mind and I know he'll be doing something similar in wild garlic season. All you need is a salted butter that you like and a big handful of wild garlic leaves.

———————

Take the butter out of the fridge and leave to soften. Meanwhile, pick your wild garlic, rinse the leaves, pat them dry and chop them quite finely. In a bowl, mix the softened butter and chopped wild garlic with a wooden spoon to blend them, then take a portion in your hand, place it on a piece of greaseproof paper and roll it into a log. Do the same with the rest of the butter so that you have 4, 6 or 8 logs. Depending on how many scallops you are cooking, keep one log aside, wrap up the others in paper and cling film and pop them in the freezer to pull out to pan-fry fillets of lemon sole, for roasting a monkfish tail, or perhaps for scallops again!

To cook the scallops in the butter, you can sear them in a pan, grill them, or place them in their shells and cook them over a fire, which is the way I like them – 1 log is enough for 8–10 scallops cooked in their shells this way. Just dot a little of the butter in the base of the shell, place the scallop on top and dot with another bit of butter. The butter will melt and will caramelise a little, possibly even burn around the shell if too close to the flame, but that all adds to the flavour of the buttery scallop which, when browned, is ready to pop in your mouth.

Herb-stuffed Baby Squid with Saffron

Serves 4–6

———

12 fresh baby squid

60g fine bulgur, rinsed and drained

2 spring onions, finely chopped

2 plump garlic cloves, finely chopped

1 tsp pul biber, Aleppo pepper, or 1 small dried red chilli, deseeded and finely chopped

2 tbsp tomato purée

1 tsp honey

3 tbsp olive oil

a generous fingerful of saffron fronds

sea salt

juice of 1 lemon

200ml white wine

a bunch of mixed garden herbs – mint, marjoram, hyssop, safe, sweet cicely – all finely chopped

freshly ground black pepper

When the local boats come into the fishing villages of Fife with a catch of baby squid, this recipe is a delicious way to enjoy them and can be adapted with different wild and garden herbs. I would serve them with fresh chanterelles sautéed in olive oil or a salad of fresh vine tomatoes seasoned with East Neuk Sea Salt. I'm using the fine bulgur available in some delicatessens, Middle Eastern stores and online, but the coarser variety found in most supermarkets will work well too.

———

Preheat the oven to 180°C (fan 160°C), 350°F, gas mark 4.

To prepare the squid, hold the body sac in one hand and pull the head off with the other. Most innards should come out with the head, but reach inside the sac with your fingers to remove any that remain in there. Whip out the transparent backbone and rinse the body sac inside and out. Pat the body sac dry and put it aside for stuffing. Sever the tentacles just above the eyes, so that you have the top of the head and the tentacle joined together. Put them aside with the sacs and discard everything else.

Put the bulgur in a bowl with the onions, garlic, pul biber, tomato purée, honey and 1 tablespoon of olive oil. Using your fingers, rub the ingredients into the bulgur grains. Leave the grains to sit for 10 minutes to absorb the flavours then pour in just enough boiling water to moisten the mixture and no more. Cover with a clean dish towel and leave the bulgur for another 10 minutes to absorb the liquid.

In a bowl, gently bash, or crumble, most of the saffron fronds (keep some whole) with a little salt and stir in 2 tablespoons of olive oil, the lemon juice and white wine. Put it aside to allow the saffron to emit its colour.

Using a fork, toss the fresh herbs into the bulgur, raking them through the grains so that they are evenly dispersed. Season the mixture to taste with salt and pepper.

Using your fingers, or a teaspoon, stuff the herby bulgur into the squid sacs – leave a little room at the top for expansion – and plug the hole with the tentacles. Place the stuffed squid into a shallow earthenware or ovenproof dish, and pour over the saffron-coloured liquid. Place the squid in the oven for about 25 minutes and serve immediately with a salad.

East Neuk Kilnhouse (St Monans)

I was obviously following in favourable footsteps when I entered the East Neuk Kilnhouse in St Monans, just around the corner from David Lowrie Fish Merchants (p.203), as a large photo of the Hairy Bikers tucking into the legendary hot-smoked salmon greeted me as I walked in the door. And I can certainly vouch for the flavour and texture of the juiciest, tastiest, hot-smoked salmon I have ever had. It is no wonder that it wins awards and that Colin Reekie, the owner of the Kilnhouse, regards it as his flagship product.

Colin has been involved in the fish merchant and manufacturing industry all of his life. Back in the 1930s, his grandfather, Charles Reekie, and great-uncle, David, skippered and co-owned the *The Honey Bee*, a steam drifter fired by coals. Colin's father, William, worked on it as a young man until he went into the merchant side of the fishing industry and set up W. Reekie Fish Merchants in Pittenweem in the 1960s. At the end of the school day, Colin would help his father wash the trays and tail the prawns and later he joined his father in the business for a while. The purchase of his own fish van took Colin on travels all over the Central Belt, meeting people and bringing fresh fish from the coast to rural communities, which he loved doing, and misses deeply, but health issues forced him to stop. But Colin isn't a man to sit about doing nothing and he saw an opportunity to buy the smokehouse, which at that time was run by his old friend Billy Morris. He kept Billy on and rebranded the business and the product; Colin's son, Calum, designed the logo using the black and gold of the local football team.

Billy has also been involved in the fishing industry and manufacturing all of his life. His father ran the smokehouse until he retired and his great-grandfather fished aboard the *Chrysophase* from St Monans until 1940. Billy starts his day in the early hours of the morning to get the fish ready for the unique, stainless-steel kiln, one of three in the world (the other two are on a cruise ship and 'somewhere in America', Billy says) which has a self-feeding firebox to produce the smoke that rises up the chimney, travels along the top and down over the fish, then changes direction so the products get evenly smoked. For the cold smoke, the sides of salmon are cured with salt and demerara sugar and smoked just over room temperature

for 8–9 hours, whereas the hot smoke takes roughly 4 hours on a gradual heat, rising every half hour. The dampened-down oak dust used in the feeder can last for 8 hours, regulating the smoke so there is no need for Billy to keep checking the fish during the process. He 'just kens with his eye' whether it's ready or not.

Aside from the cold- and hot-smoked salmon, the Kilnhouse sells succulent whole and filleted kippers (split herring), smoked mackerel, smoked haddock, smoked mussels, hot-smoked trout and some fresh fish – all available on the premises and online. Two new products reflect the business heritage: 'Auld Reekie', a maple and whisky smoked salmon, and 'The Honey Bee KY214', a honey and rum smoked salmon named after Colin's grandfather's steam drifter. KY214 was the registration number of the boat, which was built in Aberdeen in 1905 and originally fished out of Peterhead. Colin's grandfather and great uncle brought it down to St Monans where they fished for most of the year until 1937, only heading south to Yarmouth and Lowestoft in the winters for the herring.

Heritage, tradition, quality, pride and long hours of hard work are at the root of the East Neuk Kilnhouse's ethos, which is why these artisan products got the seal of approval from the Hairy Bikers.

Steamed Clappydoos
Stuffed with Aromatic Rice

Until recently, I didn't realise that clappydoos were just large mussels – too large for most culinary palates nowadays but a welcome sight in the past when poor people lived off mussels and oysters. I was reminded about them when I read Billy Connolly's autobiography, so when Colin Reekie of East Neuk Kilnhouse mentioned them I asked why we don't see them anymore and he said they are just too big. People won't eat them. So I thought I could introduce you to a delightful way of cooking them – a Turkish way – which works well with smaller mussels too.

Serves 4

———

12 large, fresh mussels, cleaned and kept in a bowl of cold water while you prepare the rice

2 tbsp olive oil

2–3 shallots, finely chopped

1 tbsp pine nuts or chopped hazelnuts

2 tbsp currants, soaked in warm water for 5 minutes, then drained

2 tsp ground cinnamon

2 tsp ground allspice

1 tsp sugar

2 tsp tomato paste

120g short grain or arborio rice, well rinsed and drained

sea salt and freshly ground black pepper

a small bunch of fresh flat-leaf parsley, finely chopped

a small bunch of fresh mint leaves, finely chopped

a small bunch of fresh dill fronds, finely chopped

lemon wedges and extra sprigs of parsley, for serving

Heat the olive oil in a heavy-based pan and stir in the shallots, until they soften. Add the pine nuts and currants. Stir for 1–2 minutes, until the pine nuts turn golden and the currants plump up. Add the cinnamon, allspice and sugar, then stir in the tomato paste. Add the rice, making sure it is well coated in the spices and paste.

Pour in enough water to just cover the rice. Season with salt and pepper and bring the water the boil. Reduce the heat, cover the pan and simmer gently until the all the water has been absorbed. Tip the rice onto a plate to cool. Toss in the fresh herbs.

Using a sharp knife, prise open each mussel shell wide enough to fill with rice. Stuff a spoonful of cooled rice into each shell, then close the shells and pack the mussels tightly into a steamer, or a colander placed in a deep pan. Lay a sheet of dampened greaseproof paper over the top of the mussels, followed by a plate weighed down with a stone (one out of the garden will do), to prevent the mussels from opening too much when steamed. Place the lid on the steamer, or pan, and bring the water to the boil. Reduce the heat and gently steam the mussels for 15–20 minutes.

Leave the mussels to cool a little in the pan. Serve them warm, or at room temperature, on a bed of parsley with lemon wedges to squeeze over them.

Pasta with Smoked Mussels, Capers and Anchovies

Smoked mussels are delicious wee morsels and fabulous in different types of paella, noodles, salads, pâtés and, of course, pasta. I swither between a light white, cream and shallot sauce reliant entirely on the smokiness of the mussels to lead the flavour and a more puttanesca style. As I'm a bit of an old tart, you can guess where I'm heading with this recipe!

Heat the olive oil with the butter in a skillet and stir in the anchovies with the rosemary and garlic until the anchovies melt and blend in. Stir in pul biber, then turn off the heat and leave to cool.

Tip the mussels into a bowl and toss in the cooled anchovy mixture with the lemon zest, lemon juice and the capers. Put aside.

Heat a pan over a high flame, tip in the breadcrumbs and toss them about the pan until they turn golden and crisp. Toss in half the parsley.

Bring a pot of water to the boil, add salt and cook the pasta shells until al dente. Drain and toss in a little olive oil. Tip in the mussel mixture and carefully toss the pasta until well coated.

Divide the pasta amongst bowls. Top with the crispy breadcrumbs, grated Parmesan and the rest of the parsley, and serve.

Serves 4

———

1 tbsp olive oil

a knob of butter

8–12 anchovy fillets, drained of oil

2–3 sprigs rosemary, finely chopped

12 plump garlic cloves, crushed

1 tsp pul biber or Aleppo pepper

200g East Neuk smoked mussels

zest and juice of 1 lemon

2 tbsp small capers in vinegar or brine, drained

sea salt and freshly ground black pepper

200g crusty loaf, ground into coarse crumbs

a small bunch of flat-leaf parsley, roughly chopped

400g conchiglie

sea salt

olive oil

4 tbsp Parmesan, finely grated

Thai Kipper Cakes
with Pineapple Sauce

Serves 4–6

For the sauce

4 shallots, peeled and chopped

2 garlic cloves, peeled and chopped

1–2 fresh red or green chillies, deseeded and chopped

1 lemongrass stalk, trimmed and chopped

a thumb-sized piece of fresh ginger, peeled and chopped

2 tbsp sesame or peanut oil

200ml coconut milk

2 tsp tamarind paste

2 tsp jaggery or muscovado sugar

2–3 slices fresh pineapple, crushed using a mortar and pestle

sea salt

roughly 350g boneless kipper fillets

1–2 tbsp Thai curry paste, red or green

2 spring onions, finely sliced

1 tbsp fish sauce

1 tbsp oyster sauce

1 large egg white

1 tbsp fresh coriander, finely chopped

vegetable oil, for frying

Most of us are familiar with fish cakes made with cod and haddock, fresh or smoked, but what about kippers? They make great fish cakes too. The filleted, boneless kippers from East Neuk Kilnhouse (p.211) are perfect for these cakes, which are delicious served with the pineapple sauce.

First prepare the sauce. Using a mortar and pestle, or a food processor, pound the shallots, garlic, chillies, lemongrass and ginger to form a paste. Heat the oil in a heavy-based pan and stir in the paste. Cook for 2–3 minutes until fragrant and beginning to colour, then stir in the coconut milk, tamarind and sugar, and bring to the boil. Beat in the crushed pineapple and simmer gently for 5 minutes. Season to taste and leave to cool.

Using a food processor, blend the kipper fillets with the curry paste until well mixed. Put the spring onions into a bowl with the fish sauce, oyster sauce, egg white and coriander. Tip in the blended fish and mix well, using your fingers to knead the mixture until it feels elastic. Then lift the mixture out of the bowl with your hands and throw it back down into the bowl. Do this several times to knock out the air.

Heat enough oil for deep-frying in a wok. Test the heat of the oil with a piece of bread first – if it sizzles and bubbles and turns crisp then you know the oil is ready. Drop a heaped teaspoon of the fish mixture into the oil to test again and then deep-fry teaspoonfuls in batches until the fish cakes are golden. Drain on kitchen paper and serve with the pineapple sauce.

Jason Byles

When Miriam Margolyes met Jayson Byles, the man behind East Neuk Seaweed, in an episode of *Lost in Scotland and Beyond* she was rather taken with his dreadlocks which he joked were from eating too much seaweed. But when I met Jayson it was one of those east-coast cold, windy, wet days so the seaweed locks were tucked under a hood as we scoured the rocks for laver. Jayson has appeared in several TV shows but his real passion is to be out foraging and sharing his knowledge – a passion that stems from his Maori heritage. It is part of who he is. He grew up with his grandparents in the New Zealand countryside where his nana cooked daily from the garden, combining vegetables with wild plants, seafood and eels from the stream. He went on to train as a chef and worked in kitchens and edible gardens for a decade and ended up as the chef in a community garden in Glasgow. It was an opportunity to manage a team of seaweed harvesters that brought Jayson to Fife and then he decided to go solo and set up East Neuk Seaweed to teach others about the fertile intertidal terrain, to harvest seasonally and respectfully, and to only take what you need as many other creatures rely on the seaweed for survival.

Jayson explained to me that the intertidal zone – where the sea meets the land – is an ever-changing environment. 'Flooded by the sea twice a day on high tides, exposed to the sun and the elements on low tides and continually harassed by the wind, sand and waves, it is a harsh environment to survive in, but a fantastic array of life flourishes in it and it is considered one of the most diverse habitats on the planet.'

The best time for foraging in the intertidal zone is when the moon and sun are in conjunction, creating low tides, known as 'spring tides' and this is when Jayson gets some of his favourite seaweeds – sea spaghetti, dabberlocks and three types of kelp. Jayson admitted that he is happiest ankle-deep in a rock pool or enjoying a fire-cooked meal beside the crashing waves so, although the weather was grim, he got his rocket stove fired up, rubbed some dried laver in a little rapeseed oil, cooked it in a pan with eggs and some chunks of moist hot-smoked salmon from East Neuk Kilnhouse (p.211), and finished it with his chef's touch of laver-infused soy sauce and sesame seeds. It was utterly delicious – and the sun came out!

Jayson's Sea Spaghetti with Chorizo, Cider and Mussels

Sea spaghetti is one of Jayson's favourite seaweeds to cook with. It's tasty, it's versatile, and in season, from mid spring to late summer, he enjoys nibbling it straight from the rocks. This recipe is Jayson's go-to at Easter as the sea spaghetti around him in the East Neuk has grown to a harvestable length and the mussels are still good to collect from the sea. And, of course, he enjoys cooking and eating this dish on the beach.

—————

Place a deep pot of seawater, or slightly salted water, on the heat and bring it to the boil.

Meanwhile, heat up a heavy-based pan and toss in the chopped chorizo for 4–5 minutes, until crisp and oily. Add the onion and garlic to the pan and fry them in the oil from the chorizo for 2 minutes. Toss in the fennel seeds, then stir in the cider and tomato purée. Season with black pepper to taste, reduce the heat and simmer for about 5 minutes until the sauce has reduced slightly.

(You can season with salt if you wish but you will probably find that the sea spaghetti provides enough salt to the dish.)

Drop the sea spaghetti into the boiling water for 8–12 minutes, depending on the firmness you prefer.

Add the mussels to the chorizo sauce. Tip in a tablespoon of cooking liquor from the sea spaghetti if the sauce is looking a little dry. Cover the pan with a lid and steam for 4–5 minutes – stir or shake the pan during this time – until all the mussels have just opened.

Drain the sea spaghetti and toss it through the mussels, making sure it gets coated in the sauce. Toss in the parsley and divide the dish between bowls. Serve with crusty bread and butter.

Serves 4–5

—————

1 large chorizo sausage, roughly chopped

1 small onion, finely sliced

3 garlic cloves, finely sliced

1 tsp fennel seeds

150ml still apple cider (leave the bottle unopened for a day)

4 tbsp tomato purée

freshly ground black pepper

400g fresh sea spaghetti cut into roughly 15–20cm lengths

roughly 2kg of fresh mussels, cleaned and debearded

a handful of flat-leaf parsley, coarsely chopped

East Neuk Salt Company (St Monans)

In 1771 Sir John Anstruther set up the Newark Coal and Salt Company in partnership with Robert Fall. They also put a lot of money into Pittenweem harbour, primarily to transport the salt needed for the booming herring industry and, on St Monans shore, they built nine saltpans into which seawater was pumped, powered by the windmill that still stands. The seawater was then heated to evaporate it and form salt crystals. Salt was produced in St Monans until 1823 and, during this time, it was Scotland's third-largest export after wool and fish.

Over 200 years later, salt is back in St Monans. Determined to preserve the past, local man Darren Peattie and his wife, Mhairi, founded the East Neuk Salt Company after walking down by the historic pans and wondering why no one in Fife was making salt anymore. To produce the salt, Darren pumps the seawater into IBC tanks in the back of a van and then takes it to the production premises where the water is left to settle naturally before it goes through a 3-set filtration process to get rid of any sand, seaweed and micro-plastics. The filtered water is then transferred into big tanks wrapped in jackets so that it evaporates under vacuum and turns into concentrated brine. It takes 6,000 litres of seawater to get 600 litres of brine which is then gravity-fed into a roof tank that feeds into the pan room (which you can see through a viewing window). Once the pan fills with this high-salinity brine, it evaporates under heat to form crystals, which are left to drain naturally before being dried in an oven. By using this method of salt making, the East Neuk Salt Company produces about 200 tons of fine salt crystal flakes a month, making them the largest producers in Scotland.

Sôlt's Baked Mackerel with
Herbs and Oak Smoked Sea Salt

Mhairi Peattie, who used to be head chef at the Dory Bistro in Pitten-weem, cooks this dish when the mackerel are running off the Isle of May, just off the coast of St Monans. She buys the mackerel straight off the boat so it is super-fresh and uses an oak-smoked version of her salt to enhance the flavour of the dish. This is a recipe she will be cooking at Sôlt, a new outside-dining experience at the East Neuk Salt Company in St Monans.

Preheat the oven to 180°C (fan 160°C), 350°F, gas mark 4.

First put all the herbs, stalks included, into a blender and blitz. Season with salt and pepper.

Using a sharp knife, make three fairly deep slashes along the topside of the mackerel and place it in an oven dish or on a foil-lined oven tray.

Season the cavity with the Oak Smoked Sea Salt and pepper. Spread a generous spoonful of the herb paste into the cavity and place a couple of lemon and orange segments and a sprig of rosemary in there too. Spread another generous spoonful of the herb paste on top of the mackerel, working it into the slashes.

Arrange the thyme sprigs on top and drizzle the olive oil over the fish. Season one more time with the Oak Smoked Sea Salt and black pepper and pop the fish in the oven for 15–20 minutes, depending on the size of the mackerel.

Enjoy the freshly baked mackerel with the rest of the citrus segments to squeeze over it and a dollop of mayonnaise or aioli, if you wish.

Serves 4

a handful of all or any of the following: parsley, dill, basil, mint and chives

East Neuk Oak Smoked Sea Salt and freshly ground black pepper

1 large mackerel, gutted, cleaned and left whole

1 lemon and 1 orange, cut into segments

a sprig of fresh rosemary

several sprigs of fresh thyme

a good glug of olive oil

Hot and Sour Mackerel and Pineapple Broth

Serves 4

For the spice paste

1 tbsp allspice berries

sea salt

4 shallots, peeled and roughly chopped

2 fresh red chillies, deseeded and roughly chopped

2 large thumb-sized pieces fresh ginger, peeled and roughly chopped

2 lemongrass stalks, trimmed and finely sliced

1 tsp shrimp paste

---

2 tbsp vegetable or peanut oil

1–2 tbsp tamarind paste

1–2 tbsp jaggery or muscovado sugar

3 pints fish or chicken stock

½ medium-sized pineapple, peeled and cut into bite-size chunks

sea salt and freshly ground black pepper

4 line-caught mackerel fillets with skin on, cut into bite-size pieces

a bunch of fresh coriander, roughly chopped

a handful of fresh mint leaves, roughly chopped

whole chillies, for garnishing (optional)

Over the years I've written about variations of this dish from Cambodia, Malaysia, West Africa, Jamaica and Louisiana, a reflection of the influences of the spice trade, the slave trade and the movement of people. Whichever influence I go for, it never ceases to be a tasty, tangy and refreshing broth. I have used mackerel in this recipe but you could use any meaty fish, such as ling, coley, halibut, sea bass, sea bream, sardines, herring or cod.

Using a mortar and pestle, pound the allspice berries with a little sea salt until powdery, then add the chopped shallots, chillies, ginger and lemongrass and pound to as smooth a paste as possible. Beat in the shrimp paste.

Heat the oil in a wok, or heavy-based pot. Stir in the spice paste and fry until fragrant. Stir in the tamarind paste and jaggery, then pour in the stock. Mix well and bring the liquid to the boil. Reduce the heat and simmer for 20 minutes.

Add the pineapple to the broth and season with salt and pepper. Adjust the sweet sourness to your taste with the tamarind and jaggery.

Add the mackerel and cook gently for 2–3 minutes, until the fish is cooked through and stir in most of the coriander and mint. Ladle the broth into bowls, garnish with the rest of the coriander and mint, add a chilli to each bowl, if you like, and serve immediately.

Belhaven Smokehouse
Hot-smoked Salmon Chowder

Originally set up as a family business in 1975 by David Pate, who had been a trout farmer in Australia, the Belhaven Smokehouse is now under new ownership, with Marie-Clare James at the helm. Working in the Scottish food industry for decades, Marie-Clare was heavily involved in the Seafood in Schools project when it launched in 2013 and is passionate about the provenance and sustainability of the products. Equally passionate about local and seasonal produce is marketing manager Meg Macfarlane who, prior to joining the smoke-house team, ran a popular supper club with her husband from their living room in Haddington, where they shone a spotlight on local food and drink businesses. Head of production, Mark Tear, has worked at the smokehouse for decades. His filleting skills are second to none and he enjoys experimenting with different cures and smoking techniques, such as Belhaven's unique charcoal-smoked salmon with its black coating contrasting the cured flesh. The charcoal coating alone accentuates the earthy taste of the salmon, which is dry-cured for 48 hours and slow-smoked for 20–24 hours. The salmon is sourced from RSPCA Assured farms in Orkney and Shetland.

Located near Dunbar, the smokehouse practises artisanal curing and smoking techniques, using specially selected oak chips, so the customers can enjoy premium, smoked fish just the way our ancestors enjoyed it.

Serves 4

---

2 tbsp Scottish rapeseed oil

25g butter

1 small leek, washed and chopped

1 small onion, finely chopped

3 large potatoes, peeled and diced

2 small (roughly 140g) tins sweetcorn

250ml vegetable or fish stock

200g Belhaven hot-smoked salmon fillets, pulled apart into chunky flakes with your fingers

250ml double cream

sea salt and freshly ground black pepper

chopped chives, for garnishing

Heat the rapeseed oil and butter in a pan and stir in the leeks and onion for 4–5 minutes to soften, until the onion is translucent.

Add the potatoes and enough boiling water to cover them, and boil until they are nearly cooked.

While the potatoes are cooking, open the tins of sweetcorn. Empty one of the tins into a blender and purée, adding a little more water if needed. Heat up the stock.

When the potatoes are nearly cooked, add the drained tin of sweetcorn, the puréed sweetcorn, the salmon flakes and the warm stock, and continue to heat through.

Add the cream, season to taste with salt and pepper and garnish with the chives. Serve hot with crusty bread.

Belhaven Lobster (Dunbar)

The *Tangaroa*, named after the Maori god of the sea, can often be spotted in the Dunbar's Victoria Harbour in East Lothian. It is the primary fishing vessel of Belhaven Lobster, which is owned by father and son Eddie and Lawrie McFarlane, and its name is a reminder of their ties to New Zealand. It is equipped with the latest seabed mapping technology as well as an onboard seawater sprinkler system to keep the catch fresh on deck. The primary catch is lobster and brown crab, which skipper Lawrie and crewman Craig Darling target in the rocky waters surrounding Dunbar and up to six miles offshore, usually within sight of Belhaven Bay. This is done by deploying fleets of lobster pots (creels), which are hauled on board and emptied on a daily basis throughout the year. The catch is transferred to the company's innovative seawater storage system which ensures that it is kept at an optimal temperature with an uninterrupted supply of oxygenated water and in low-level light to reduce stress levels and retain the quality of the meat. Eddie tells me, 'A lot has changed over the years with the advances in technology used in the fishing, but essentially we are using the same methods that have been used for hundreds of years.'

For decades the catch was loaded onto a truck and distributed across Europe, but the fishing industry was hit hard by both Brexit and the pandemic lockdowns, so Eddie and Lawrie McFarlane decided to sell local, within a 50-mile radius, to restaurants in Edinburgh and from the deck of their boat to customers in East Lothian. It is a decision they don't regret as they can get to know their customers and chat about the quantity they need and what they are going to cook with it.

This engagement with customers also provides Eddie and Lawrie with an opportunity to inform them about Belhaven Lobster's commitment to improving the sustainability of fishing in the area. Lawrie says, 'We try to fish in a responsible way to limit the impact our fishing methods have on the seabed whilst also giving the lobsters a chance to repopulate by returning all non-suitable ones to the sea.'

It is an issue they feel strongly about.

Belhaven Lobster Chargrilled with Garlicky Harissa and Coriander Butter

Serves 2

120g softened butter

2 garlic cloves, crushed

1 tsp harissa paste

grated zest of 1 lemon (keep the lemon for squeezing)

a small bunch of fresh coriander, finely chopped

sea salt

1 medium-sized lobster, kept at –1°C to stun it into hibernation before cooking

Eddie and Lawrie McFarlane may be ready to go out in the 'God of the Sea' in all weathers to keep up a consistent supply of lobsters but, when it comes to preparing lobsters to eat, Lawrie confesses he's not much of a cook. So, I have suggested this simple idea for him to cook on one of the lovely beaches near Dunbar where he can still enjoy the sea.

Before heading to the beach, or cooking over a grill in your garden, prepare the lobster. Place the lobster in the freezer for 10 minutes so that it goes into a numb state. Then, using a sharp knife, cut though the head quickly and cut it in half lengthways. Remove the digestive tract and crack the shell of the claws with the back of your knife. If you're heading to the beach, pack the lobster meat and claws into a container to take with you.

Get your barbeque, or grill, hot and ready.

Tip the softened butter into a bowl and beat in the crushed garlic and harissa paste. Add the lemon zest and half the coriander and season with a little salt.

Spread the butter over the lobster meat and claws and place them over the barbeque, or under the grill, for about 20 minutes, until tender and lightly browned.

Serve hot with a squeeze of lemon and an extra sprinkling of coriander.

Spicy Fish Tacos or Wraps with Neep Pickles, Tartare Potatoes and Guacamole Salsa

Let's get messy! This is one for the family. Tacos, wraps and filled, toasted pitta breads were always a great favourite when my kids were growing up as you can put pretty much anything into them and make them as punchy and personal as you like. So, here I have suggested some accompaniments to go with spicy fish so that you can enjoy assembling your own – a great way to get the kids to enjoy fish! Use any sustainably caught, chunky white fish and shop-bought wraps, tacos, pitta bread or baps. Assemble the pickles, potatoes, salsa and extras before frying the fish and enjoying the flavours and the mess!

To make the neep pickles, mix all the ingredients together in a bowl and leave to sit for 1–2 hours.

For the tartare potatoes, first make the tartare dressing. Combine the oil with the vinegar, mustard and soured cream and season to taste.

Boil the potatoes in plenty water until tender, but still have a bite to them. Drain and break, or roughly cut, into small chunks and toss in the dressing and shallots while still warm, making sure you coat the potatoes. Toss in the capers, gherkins and fresh herbs.

To make the guacamole salsa, bring a small pot of water to the boil. Drop in the tomatoes for 20–30 seconds, then drain and refresh under cold water. This helps to separate the flesh from the skin, which you can pull off with your fingers. Halve the tomatoes, scrape out the seeds, and dice the flesh.

Tip the tomatoes into a bowl with the onion, avocados, and chillies. Combine the lime juice with the crushed garlic and coriander, season with salt and pepper and pour it over the salad. Toss well.

Once you have prepared and assembled all the pickles, salsa, sauces and extras on the table, you can fry the fish.

Tip the flour into a shallow bowl and mix well with the salt and most of the ground spices and chilli flakes – add the rest to the beaten eggs.

Serves 4–6

For the fish

3 tbsp fine maize flour, or fine plain wholemeal flour

½ tsp sea salt

1 tsp ground cumin

1 tsp ground coriander

1 tsp ground turmeric

1 tsp pul biber, Aleppo pepper, or dried chilli flakes

2 eggs, beaten

sunflower or vegetable oil, for frying

600g meaty white fish fillets, with skin removed and cut into chunks

------

For the neep pickles

1 carrot, julienned

250g turnip, julienned

6–8 red radishes, finely sliced

200ml rice wine vinegar

1 tbsp agave syrup

1 tsp sea salt

229

For the tartare potatoes

1 tbsp olive oil

1 tbsp white wine or cider vinegar

1 tsp Dijon mustard

2 tbsp soured cream

sea salt and freshly ground black pepper

450g waxy salad or new potatoes

1–2 shallots, finely chopped

2 tbsp soured cream

1 tbsp capers in vinegar, drained

roughly 6–8 small gherkins, finely chopped

a small bunch of chives, parsley and dill, all finely chopped together

———

For the guacamole salsa

2 large tomatoes,

1 red onion, finely chopped

2 avocados, skinned, stoned and diced

1–2 green chillies, deseeded and finely chopped

juice of 2 limes

2 garlic cloves, crushed

a bunch of fresh coriander, finely chopped

sea salt and freshly ground black pepper

Heat a thin layer of oil in a frying pan. Toss the pieces of fish in the flour, shaking off any excess. Dip them into the beaten egg, dripping off any excess, and then place in the oil in the pan. Fry the fish in batches and drain on kitchen towel. Now assemble your tacos or wraps.

Extras

1 gem lettuce, shredded
cherry tomatoes, halved or quartered
cheddar cheese, coarsely grated (optional)
pickled cucumbers
soured cream, crème fraiche, or yoghurt
chilli sauce, chipotle paste or Tabasco
a bunch of fresh coriander, roughly chopped
12 shop-bought tacos, wraps or pitta breads

INDEX OF RECIPES

INDEX